The History of Israel

Myths, Facts, and the Jewish Story Revealed

FREE BONUS FROM HBA: EBOOK BUNDLE

Greetings!

First, thank you for reading our books.

Now, we invite you to join our VIP list. As a welcome gift we offer the History & Mythology eBook Bundle below for free. Plus, you can be the first to receive new books and exclusives! Remember it's 100% free to join.

Simply click the link below to join.

https://www.subscribepage.com/hba
Keep up to date with us on:
YouTube: History Brought Alive
Facebook: History Brought Alive
www.historybroughtalive.com

TABLE OF CONTENTS

Introduction

Throughout human history, numerous civilizations and cultures have been misunderstood. They were often subjected to hostile scrutiny, bias, and misinterpretation. Such is the tale of Israel, which is seldom dissected from a strictly historical standpoint. The history of Israel is crisscrossed with ancient civilizations, religious narratives, and the enduring quest for national identity. It is a nation that has been at the heart of historical events that have shaped the world, yet understanding its ancient past remains a challenge. Israel's history spans thousands of years, involves numerous cultures, and has been a focal point for religious and political developments. For many, the sheer volume of information, coupled with diverse interpretations, makes it difficult to grasp the full scope of Israel's past.

In these pages, we will address that challenge by presenting a comprehensive and accessible account of the history of Israel, from its ancient origins to contemporary times. By weaving together archaeological discoveries, historical documentation, and theological insights, this work aims to present an accurate historical narrative. The core of our work is anchored in rigorous research and consultation with experts in the fields of archaeology, history, and theology. By considering both the archaeological and Biblical sources, we can bridge the gap between academic scholarship and public understanding, making the intricate history of Israel accessible to a broad audience.

On this journey, we will be introduced to the diverse cultures and peoples that have inhabited the land of Israel. From the Canaanites and Philistines to the Israelites and Judeans, we will explore the unique contributions and influences of these groups. We will also delve into the profound impact of religious traditions, from the beliefs of the ancient Israelites to the emergence of Christianity and Islam, and how these faiths have shaped the cultural and spiritual landscape of Israel.

The narrative will also explore the complex interplay between power and faith, as well as the role of Israel as a crossroads of civilizations. This nation has been a focal point for empires and conquerors, from the Egyptians and Babylonians to the Greeks and Romans. It has witnessed the rise and fall of kingdoms and the birth of new ideologies and movements. By examining these historical developments, readers will gain a deeper appreciation of the resilience of the people who have called this land home.

This book highlights the interconnectedness of history, religion, and politics. Understanding the historical context of current events gives readers a better perspective on the complexities of the modern Middle East. We encourage readers to consider the lessons of the past and their relevance to current and future challenges. As we examine the historical roots of current issues, we provide a foundation for informed discussion and dialogue. We invite readers to consider the importance of historical awareness in shaping a more just and peaceful future.

Chapter 1
The Prehistory of the Levant
and the History of Canaan

The area that we know today as Israel has been the focal point of cultural development since the dawn of civilization. The entire region of the Levant – that is, the core territory of the political term "Middle East" – was always a bustling crossroad where numerous cultures, ethnicities, and civilizations met. The area was therefore fertile ground for human evolution, adaptation, and cultural blooming. A knowledge of the prehistoric period of the Levant is crucial for understanding the later emergence of the Israelites and the laying of the foundations of Israel.

The **Lower Paleolithic Era** (ca. 1.5 million to 250,000 years ago) marks the earliest evidence of human activity in the Levant. Sites such as Ubeidiya near the Sea of Galilee and Gesher Benot Ya'aqov in the Jordan Valley provide crucial insights into the lives of Homo erectus, an early human species that inhabited the region. Ubeidiya, in particular, throws light on the early movements of our shared ancestors. This site is around 1.4 million years old and is one of the oldest archaeological sites outside of Africa, showcasing the migration of early hominids. An array of crude stone tools, such as hand axes and flake tools, has been discovered at the site, indicating that the early hominids had some technological capabilities.

Similarly, the site at Gesher Benot Ya'aqov dates to approximately 780,000 years ago and offers further evidence of early human ingenuity. The site reveals a rich assemblage of Acheulean tools, including hand axes and cleavers, as well as evidence of the controlled use of fire. The presence of charred wood and seeds suggests that these early humans were able to harness fire for cooking and warmth, a significant milestone in human evolution. Additionally, the site indicates a diverse diet, including plant material, fish, and large mammals, demonstrating a broad spectrum of subsistence strategies. According to archaeologists from the Hebrew University of Jerusalem, the site displays advanced human behavior some 500,000 years earlier than originally thought.

The **Middle Paleolithic** (ca. 250,000 to 50,000 years ago) in the Levant is characterized by the presence of both Neanderthals and Early Modern

Humans (Homo sapiens). This is a period marked by significant advances in tool technology and the emergence of complex social behaviors. Two major discoveries, in Tabun Cave and Skhul Cave in the Mount Carmel range, provide invaluable evidence of human activity during this era.

Tabun Cave, part of the Nahal Me'arot Nature Reserve, contains a sequence of archaeological layers spanning hundreds of thousands of years. Excavations at this site revealed a variety of stone tools, such as Levallois flakes and Mousterian points, commonly associated with Neanderthals. Also found at the site was a Neanderthal burial, which provides rare insights into the mortuary practices of these early humans.

Located nearby is Skhul Cave, which similarly offers evidence of early modern human occupation. The site contains skeletal remains of Homo sapiens dating to around 100,000 years ago, making it one of the oldest known sites of modern human habitation outside of Africa. The presence of shell beads and ochre at Skhul suggests that these early humans engaged in symbolic behavior, possibly indicating the development of early forms of art and personal adornment.

During the **Upper Paleolithic Era** (ca. 50,000 to 10,000 years ago), the Levant region witnessed significant technological and cultural advancements, including the development of more sophisticated tools and the emergence of art. A major archeological site from this period is Kebara Cave on Mount Carmel, which provided a window into the lives of Upper Paleolithic Era humans in the Levant. Upon discovery, it yielded a rich array of artifacts, including blade tools and bone implements, and evidence of advanced fire use. The discovery of a well-preserved burial, known as Kebara 2, provided valuable evidence of the funerary practices and physical characteristics of people of this era. This site, too, revealed considerable evidence of a diverse diet, including plant material, fish, and large mammals.

(Image: Kebara 2 skeleton replica, Public Domain)

Furthermore, the presence of symbolic artifacts, such as beads and incised bones, suggests that Upper Paleolithic humans in the Levant engaged in complex social and cultural behaviors. These early humans likely developed intricate social networks and communication systems, laying the groundwork for the more complex societies that would emerge in the Neolithic era.

Life after the Neolithic Revolution

The subsequent **Neolithic Revolution** (ca. 10,000 to 4,500 BC) marked a major transformation in human societies around the world. This era was characterized by a transition from a hunter-gatherer lifestyle to settled agricultural communities. It also saw the domestication of plants and animals, the establishment of permanent villages and fortified communities, and the development of complex social structures. The area of the Levant played a significant role in this transformation.

One of the most significant Neolithic sites in this region is Jericho, located in the Jordan Valley. Jericho is often considered one of the oldest continuously inhabited cities in the world, with evidence of settlement dating back to around 10,000 BC. Archeological excavations at Jericho have revealed a well-developed community with substantial stone walls and towers, suggesting a high level of social organization and communal effort. The early inhabitants of this city cultivated crops such as wheat and barley, and domesticated animals such as sheep and goats. The surplus food production allowed for population growth and the emergence of specialized crafts and trade.

We also have to mention the abundance of discoveries at Jericho. They include pottery, various tools, everyday items, and artistic figures and provide valuable insights into the daily lives and cultural practices of Neolithic inhabitants of this town. The presence of vast burial sites and ritual objects also indicates the development of religious and ceremonial practices, suggesting that the people of ancient Jericho had complete belief systems and social hierarchies. All this laid the foundations of culture for subsequent tribes, including the Israelites.

Other notable Neolithic sites in the Levant are Einan (Ain Mallaha) in the Upper Jordan Valley and Beisamoun in the Hula Valley. Einan, dating to around 10,000 BC, is one of the earliest known permanent villages in the region. The site revealed evidence of circular stone houses, storage facilities, and a diverse diet that included wild cereals, legumes, and game animals. The inhabitants of

Einan practiced a mixed economy, combining hunting and gathering with early forms of cultivation.

Beisamoun provides further evidence of the transition to an agrarian lifestyle. The site features rectangular houses with plastered floors, storage pits, and an array of tools and artifacts. The discovery of sickle blades and grinding stones at the site suggests that the inhabitants engaged in cereal cultivation and food processing. Beisamoun also contains burial sites and ceremonial items, indicating the development of social and religious practices.

Following this was the gradual shift towards the Chalcolithic Period, also known as the **Copper Age** (ca. 4500 to 3500 BC). This represents a transitional phase between the Neolithic and the Bronze Age. During this time, the use of copper tools and artifacts began to complement stone tools, leading to significant advancements in technology and craftsmanship. The Copper Age is further characterized by the development of more complex societies and the establishment of much larger settlements.

One of the most important of such settlements in the Levant is called En Gedi, located near the Dead Sea. Excavations here have uncovered a well-planned village with rectangular houses, storage facilities, and public buildings. The discovery of sophisticated copper tools and artifacts, including decorative items and religious objects, highlights the technological advances of the Chalcolithic period. The inhabitants of En Gedi practiced a mixed economy, combining agriculture with pastoralism and trade. The presence of exotic materials such as obsidian and seashells indicates extensive trade networks that connected En Gedi with distant regions. The site also features a unique temple complex, suggesting the development of religious and ceremonial practices.

Other notable Chalcolithic sites in the Levant are Shiqmim in the northern Negev and Teleilat Ghassul in the Jordan Valley. Shiqmim, dating to around 4000 BC, provides evidence of a large village with well-constructed houses, storage facilities, and workshops. The discovery of copper tools and artifacts indicates that the inhabitants of Shiqmim were skilled metallurgists, engaged in the production and trade of copper items. The site also contains burial sites and religious objects, suggesting the development of social and religious practices.

The site at Teleilat Ghassul, which is located near the Jordan River, is one of the most important

Chalcolithic sites in the entire region. It features a well-planned village with rectangular houses, storage facilities, and public buildings. The discovery of sophisticated pottery, tools, and artifacts, including decorative items and religious objects, highlights the technological and cultural advancements of the Chalcolithic period. The inhabitants of Teleilat Ghassul engaged in agriculture, pastoralism, and trade, indicating a complex and diverse economy, which gives us a glimpse into the development of the region.

On the whole, the Chalcolithic period in the Levant represents a crucial phase in the development of human societies. It was characterized by significant technological advancements and the emergence of more complex social structures. The use of copper tools and artifacts, along with the establishment of larger settlements and trade networks, set the stage for the rise of the Bronze Age civilizations that would dominate the region in the following millennia.

During the **Early Bronze Age** (ca. 3500 to 2000 BC) in the territory of modern Israel, a process of urbanization began, as well as the emergence of the first city-states. The period is characterized by the development of writing, the construction of monumental architecture, and the establishment of complex political and economic systems. One of the most important Early Bronze Age sites in the Levant is the city of Megiddo, located in the Jezreel Valley. Megiddo was a major center of trade and administration, strategically positioned at the crossroads of key trade routes. Excavations at Megiddo have revealed impressive fortifications, palaces, and temples, reflecting the city's political and economic significance. The inhabitants of Megiddo engaged in agriculture, trade, and craft production. The discovery of numerous artifacts, including pottery, tools, and inscriptions, provides valuable insights into the daily life and cultural practices of the Early Bronze Age inhabitants. The presence of imported goods such as Egyptian pottery and Mesopotamian cylinder seals indicates extensive trade connections with neighboring regions. Other notable Early Bronze Age sites in the Levant are Arad in the Negev Desert and Ai in the central hill country. These settlements provide further evidence of the development of urban centers and the establishment of complex social and political structures. The Early Bronze Age represents a period of significant cultural and technological advancements, setting the stage for the subsequent Middle Bronze Age civilizations.

The History of Canaan

Situated at the crossroads of Africa, Asia, and Europe, the region of Canaan – comprising modern-day Israel, Palestine, Lebanon, and parts of Syria and Jordan – served as a melting pot of civilizations. Today, Canaanites are generally considered to be the earliest ancestors of the later Israelites. Renowned biblical scholar Mark Smith, backing his work with extensive archeological evidence, states the following:

> Despite the long regnant model that the Canaanites and Israelites were people of fundamentally different culture, archaeological data now casts doubt on this view. The material culture of the region exhibits numerous common points between Israelites and Canaanites in the Iron I period (c. 1200–1000 BC). The record would suggest that the Israelite culture largely overlapped with and derived from Canaanite culture... In short, Israelite culture was largely Canaanite in nature. Given the information available, one cannot maintain a radical cultural separation between Canaanites and Israelites for the Iron I period. (Smith, 2002)

The earliest references to Canaan come from ancient texts, including the Bible and Egyptian inscriptions. Here, the term "Canaan" is used to describe the land and its inhabitants in what is today the Levant. Archaeological evidence suggests that the Canaanites were part of a broader cultural and ethnic group known as the Northwest Semites, who inhabited the Levant during the third millennium BC. Canaan's strategic location along major trade routes connecting Egypt, Mesopotamia, and the Mediterranean made it a hub of commerce and cultural exchange. The region's fertile plains and coastal areas supported agriculture, while its proximity to the Mediterranean Sea facilitated maritime trade. These factors contributed to the early development of urban centers and the emergence of complex societies.

By the Early Bronze Age (ca. 3500-2000 BC), Canaan had developed into a region of walled cities and city-states, each governed by local rulers. Notable city-states included Jericho, Megiddo, Hazor, and Byblos. These cities were characterized by their impressive fortifications, public buildings, and intricate water systems. All of this reflects a high degree of social organization and technological prowess.

Jericho, one of the oldest continuously inhabited cities in the world, provides a glimpse into the early urbanization of Canaan. Archaeological excavations have revealed massive stone walls, a tower, and evidence of advanced agricultural practices. The city's strategic location near the Jordan River allowed it to control trade routes and access to water resources.

Similarly, Megiddo, another prominent city-state, played a crucial role in Canaan's history due to its strategic position at the intersection of major trade routes. The city's extensive archaeological remains include palaces, temples, and an elaborate water system. Megiddo's significance is underscored by its frequent mention in ancient texts, including Egyptian and Mesopotamian records.

Hazor, located in the Upper Galilee, was one of the largest and most powerful city-states in Canaan. Excavations here have uncovered monumental architecture, including a massive palace and a sophisticated water supply system. The city's wealth and influence are reflected in the abundance of luxury goods and imported artifacts found at the site.

Byblos, situated on the Mediterranean coast, was a major center of trade and shipbuilding. The city is renowned for its connections with ancient Egypt, as evidenced by the presence of Egyptian artifacts and inscriptions. Byblos played a key role in the export of cedar wood, a highly prized commodity in the ancient world.

Image: (The name "Canaan" in Egyptian hieroglyphics)
(Image: KAnana, Public Domain)

Religion was a central aspect of Canaanite society, influencing various aspects of daily life and governance. The Canaanites practiced a polytheistic religion, worshiping a pantheon of gods and goddesses associated with natural elements, fertility, and warfare. Key deities included *El*, the chief god; *Baal*, the storm god; *Asherah*, the mother goddess; and *Astarte*, the goddess of fertility and love. Temples and sanctuaries dedicated to these deities were common in Canaanite cities. These religious structures often served as the focal points of urban life, hosting various rituals, sacrifices, and festivals. The discovery of cultic objects, such as figurines, altars, and inscribed tablets, provides valuable insights into the religious practices and beliefs of the Canaanites. Their religious system was closely linked to their agricultural economy. Fertility rites and seasonal festivals were conducted to ensure the prosperity of crops and livestock. They believed that their gods controlled the natural forces and, therefore, sought to appease them through offerings and rituals.

Canaanite culture was also marked by significant contributions to art, literature, and technology. The development of the proto-Canaanite script, an early form of writing, laid the foundation for the later Phoenician alphabet, which influenced the writing systems of the Greeks and Romans. Canaanite art and craftsmanship are evident in the intricate pottery, metalwork, and jewelry discovered at various archaeological sites.

Canaan's geographic location positioned it as a critical link between the great civilizations of Egypt and Mesopotamia, as well as the emerging cultures of the Mediterranean, such as the Hittites and the Mycenaeans. The discovery of Mycenaean pottery in Canaanite archaeological sites indicates active trade and cultural interactions between the two regions. The Canaanites engaged in both overland and maritime trade, exporting commodities such as timber, olive oil, wine, textiles, and pottery in return for luxury goods, metals, and raw materials. The extensive trade networks established by the Canaanites contributed to their economic prosperity and cultural exchange.

One of the most striking features of the Late Bronze Age was the rise of "internationalism", which had begun during the Middle Bronze Age but reached new heights in the mid-second millennium. Vast exchange networks, channeling both luxury items, such as wine, and industrial goods, such as timber and metals, were in operation throughout the eastern Mediterranean. The material culture of Late Bronze Age Canaan, in addition to texts found in this and adjacent regions, indicates regular commercial interaction with people of Cyprus and the Aegean. It also reflects the infiltration of such people, along with Egyptians and Hurrians, into various parts of the Levant. (Golden, 2009)

Canaan and Egypt

We must note that the history of Canaan is closely intertwined with that of ancient Egypt. During the latter's Middle Kingdom period (ca. 2040-1782 BC), Egyptian influence in Canaan began to grow, marked by increased trade and military expeditions. The Egyptians sought to control the lucrative trade routes and access to resources in Canaan. All this led to periodic campaigns and the establishment of their garrisons in the region. The New Kingdom period (ca. 1550-1077 BC) saw a more concerted effort by Egypt to dominate neighboring Canaan. Pharaohs such as Thutmose III and Ramses II conducted military campaigns to subdue the Canaanite city-states and integrate them into the Egyptian empire. This led to prolonged conflicts.

The Battle of Megiddo, fought by Thutmose III in the 15th century BC against the Canaanites, is one of the earliest recorded battles in history. It highlights the strategic importance of Canaan on the world stage of that period. Egyptian rule over this region was characterized by the imposition of tribute, the establishment of administrative centers, and the strong presence of Egyptian officials. Despite Egyptian dominance, however, the Canaanite city-states maintained a degree of autonomy and continued to flourish. The influence of Egyptian culture is evident in the adoption of Egyptian artistic styles, religious practices, and administrative methods. Nevertheless, the Canaanites also retained their distinct cultural identity, blending Egyptian elements with their indigenous traditions.

The Egyptian Amarna Period (ca. 1353-1336 BC) was a tumultuous time in the history of Canaan, marked by significant political and social upheaval. The correspondence between the controversial Egyptian pharaoh Akhenaten and the rulers of Canaan was preserved in the Amarna Letters, written on clay tablets. They reveal a region embroiled in turmoil, plagued by internal conflicts and external threats. One of the major threats during this period was the arrival of the enigmatic Sea Peoples. These were a confederation of maritime raiders of largely unknown provenance, who attacked and destabilized coastal cities across the eastern Mediterranean. The invasion of the Sea Peoples contributed to the widespread destruction and collapse of several Canaanite city-states, leading to a period of major decline and instability.

What followed was the **Late Bronze Age collapse** (ca. 1200 BC), a period of widespread upheaval and the end of many ancient civilizations, including those in Canaan. The reasons for this collapse are complex and multifaceted, involving factors such as natural disasters, climate change, and internal strife. On top of it all came the invasions by external groups such as the infamous Sea Peoples. But despite the collapse of many city-states, some Canaanite settlements managed to survive and adapt to the changing circumstances. The resilience of these communities laid the groundwork for the emergence of new political entities in the Iron Age, including the kingdoms of Israel and Judah. And, by the mid-10th century BC, the Canaanite speakers would coalesce into a number of smaller polities, chiefly Israel, Moab, Edom, and Ammon.

The relationship between the Canaanites and the emerging Hebrew tribes is a central theme in the history of ancient Israel. The Hebrew Bible, particularly the books of Joshua and Judges, describes the conquest of Canaan by the Israelites under the leadership of Joshua. According to biblical accounts, the Israelites conducted a series of military campaigns to conquer and settle in the land of Canaan. Archaeological evidence, however, provides a more nuanced picture of the interactions between the Canaanites and the Israelites. Rather than a swift and total conquest, the process appears to have been gradual and involved a mix of conflict, assimilation, and coexistence. The Israelites adopted many aspects of Canaanite culture, including their language, agricultural practices, and religious traditions. The two "tribes" shared a common Semitic heritage, which facilitated cultural exchange and assimilation. Over time, the distinct identity of the Canaanites began to merge with that of the Israelites, contributing to the development of a new, unified culture in the region.

Because of this, the history of Canaan is crucial in the overall history of Israel. The Canaanites' contributions to art, writing, and technology laid the foundation for subsequent civilizations, including the Phoenicians and the Israelites. The Phoenicians, who emerged from the Canaanite city-states along the Mediterranean coast, were renowned for their maritime prowess and the development of the Phoenician alphabet. This writing system, derived from the proto-Canaanite script, became the basis for the Greek and Latin alphabets, profoundly impacting the development of writing and literacy in the Western world. The religious traditions of the Canaanites also left a lasting mark on the region. Many of the deities and religious practices of the Canaanites were incorporated into the emerging Israelite religion. The worship of Baal and Asherah, for example, is frequently mentioned in the Hebrew Bible, reflecting the syncretic nature of ancient religious practices.

Chapter 2
The Israelites: Their Origins
and Early History

The origins of the Israelites are a subject of considerable scholarly debate, as they are intertwined with biblical narratives and archaeological findings. The Hebrew Bible presents the Israelites as descendants of the patriarchs Abraham, Isaac, and Jacob, who settled in the land of Canaan. According to biblical tradition, the Israelites were enslaved in Egypt before being led to freedom by Moses in the Exodus. They eventually settled in the land promised to them by God.

What we know from history, however, is that the Israelite tribes first appeared on the world stage following the tumultuous period of the Late Bronze Age collapse and the ultimate waning of Canaan. Gradually they settled in the Levant, building their villages and establishing a foothold. Along with the Philistines and Phoenicians, the Israelites thus became "successors" of disappearing Canaan.

Archaeological surveys and excavations in the central hill country of Canaan have revealed a pattern of small, rural settlements dating to the early **Iron Age** (ca. 1200-1000 BC). These settlements, characterized by simple, unfortified structures and a subsistence economy, suggest the presence of a decentralized, agrarian society. The lack of pig bones in these settlements, along with the distinctive pottery styles, supports the hypothesis that these communities were culturally distinct from the surrounding Canaanite populations. Thus, the emergence of the Israelites in this period is thought to be the result of a combination of factors. These include the gradual infiltration of semi-nomadic groups into the highlands, the collapse of Canaanite city-states, and the development of a distinct identity rooted in shared religious and cultural practices. This process of ethnogenesis laid the foundation for the later formation of a unified Israelite state, leading to the emergence of Israelite identity.

> It is probably… during Iron Age I [that] a population began to identify itself as "Israelite", differentiating itself from its neighbors via prohibitions on intermarriage, an emphasis on family history and genealogy, and religion. (McNutt, 1999)

The relationship between the early Israelites and ancient Egypt is a critical aspect of Israel's formative history. The biblical narrative of the Exodus describes the Israelites' escape from Egyptian bondage and their subsequent journey to the Promised Land. While the historicity of the Exodus remains a topic of debate, Egypt's influence on the region during this period is well-documented. Following the decline of the Egyptian New Kingdom in the 11th century BC, Egypt's control over Canaan waned. This created a power vacuum that allowed emerging groups such as the Israelites to establish themselves in the region.

However, Egyptian influence persisted, as evidenced by the presence of Egyptian artifacts and inscriptions in Canaanite and early Israelite sites. One of the most significant pieces of evidence linking the Israelites to Egypt is the Merneptah Stele, dating to around 1208 BC. This stele, erected by famed Pharaoh Merneptah, contains the earliest extra-biblical reference to Israel, mentioning a campaign in Canaan and stating, "Israel is laid waste; its seed is no more." The stele is evidence that a group identified as "Israel" existed in Canaan by the late 13th century BC. This indicates a complex interplay between the Israelites and their Egyptian neighbors. Even by this time, the

Israelites were formidable enough to be seen by the Egyptians as a challenge.

The following period of the **United Monarchy** represents a critical juncture in the history of ancient Israel. It marks the transition from a loosely organized confederation of tribes to a centralized state. According to the biblical narrative, this era began with the anointing of a prominent leader, Saul, as the first king of Israel. His reign was followed by the reigns of David and Solomon, who established Jerusalem as the political and religious center of the kingdom. Saul, from the tribe of Benjamin, was chosen as the first king of Israel around 1050 BC. His reign is depicted in the biblical books of Samuel as a time of consolidation and conflict. Saul's primary challenge was to unify the disparate tribes of Israel and defend them against external threats, particularly the Philistines. These neighbors controlled the coastal plains and posed a significant military threat. While Saul achieved some success in his military campaigns, his reign was marked by internal strife and struggles for power. The biblical account portrays Saul as a tragic figure whose inability to fully unite the tribes and maintain divine favor ultimately led to his downfall. His reign ended in a disastrous battle against the neighboring Philistines at Mount Gilboa, where he and his sons were killed.

Following Saul's death, David, a young shepherd from the tribe of Judah, rose to prominence. The biblical narrative describes David as a charismatic and capable leader who established himself as king over Judah and later united all of Israel under his rule. David's military prowess and strategic alliances enabled him to expand Israel's territory and secure its borders.

David's most significant achievement was the capture of Jerusalem, which he established as the capital of the United Monarchy. Jerusalem's central location and defensible position made it an ideal political and religious center. David's reign is often regarded as a golden age in Israel's history, characterized by military victories, territorial expansion, and the establishment of a centralized administration.

David's son Solomon succeeded him, inheriting a united and prosperous kingdom. Solomon's reign, traditionally dated to around 970-931 BC, is depicted as a time of unparalleled wealth, cultural flourishing, and diplomatic achievements. Under Solomon, Israel reached the height of its power and influence. One of Solomon's most enduring legacies was the construction of the First Temple in Jerusalem, a monumental undertaking that solidified the city's status as the religious heart of

Israel. According to the biblical account, the Temple was built on Mount Moriah, the site where Abraham was said to have prepared to sacrifice his son Isaac. The Temple served as the central place of worship for the Israelites and housed the Ark of the Covenant. Solomon's reign was also marked by extensive building projects, including palaces, fortifications, and infrastructure improvements. His administration fostered trade and diplomatic relations with neighboring states, such as Egypt and Phoenicia, enhancing Israel's economic and cultural standing. However, Solomon's reign was not without controversy. The biblical narrative highlights his extensive network of alliances through marriage, including foreign wives who introduced their own religious practices to Israel. Additionally, the heavy taxation and forced labor required for his ambitious building projects created discontent among the populace, sowing the seeds for future divisions.

After Solomon's death, the united kingdom he had built began to unravel. The tensions that had simmered during his reign erupted into open conflict, leading to the division of Israel into two separate kingdoms: Israel in the north and Judah in the south. This division marked the end of the United Monarchy and set the stage for a new era in Israel's history. This era was characterized by political instability, prophetic voices, and external threats. However, it is important to note that some scholars dispute the actual existence of the United Monarchy for lack of archaeological evidence. It is, however, generally agreed that it did exist in some shape or form, possibly smaller than described in the Hebrew Bible.

The Two Kingdoms: Judah and Israel

The unity achieved during the reigns of Saul, David, and Solomon was short-lived. After Solomon's death around 931 BC, internal strife and social unrest led to the division of the Israelite kingdom. It now constituted two separate entities: the northern Kingdom of Israel and the southern Kingdom of Judah. This division was precipitated by a combination of economic grievances, tribal rivalries, and political ambitions. Solomon's son, Rehoboam, ascended to the throne, but his reign was quickly challenged by Jeroboam. Jeroboam was a former official in Solomon's administration who capitalized on popular discontent. The northern tribes, frustrated by the heavy taxation and forced labor imposed by Solomon, rebelled against Rehoboam's authority and declared their independence. Jeroboam was crowned king of the newly formed northern kingdom, which retained the name Israel, while Rehoboam remained the ruler of Judah, centered around Jerusalem. The division of the kingdom had profound political and religious implications for the region. The northern Kingdom of Israel, with its capital initially at Shechem and later at Samaria, was larger and more populous than Judah but struggled with political instability and external threats. The southern Kingdom of Judah, though smaller, maintained control over Jerusalem and the Temple, giving it a significant religious advantage.

The divided kingdoms of Israel and Judah experienced varying degrees of stability and prosperity, often influenced by their interactions with neighboring powers such as Egypt, Assyria, and Aram-Damascus. The political landscape of the region during this period was characterized by shifting alliances, intermittent warfare, and the rise and fall of dynasties. By the first half of the 9th century BC, however, the Kingdom of Israel was consolidated and emerged as a regional power. Similarly, the neighboring Kingdom of Judah began flourishing in the second half of the 9th century BC.

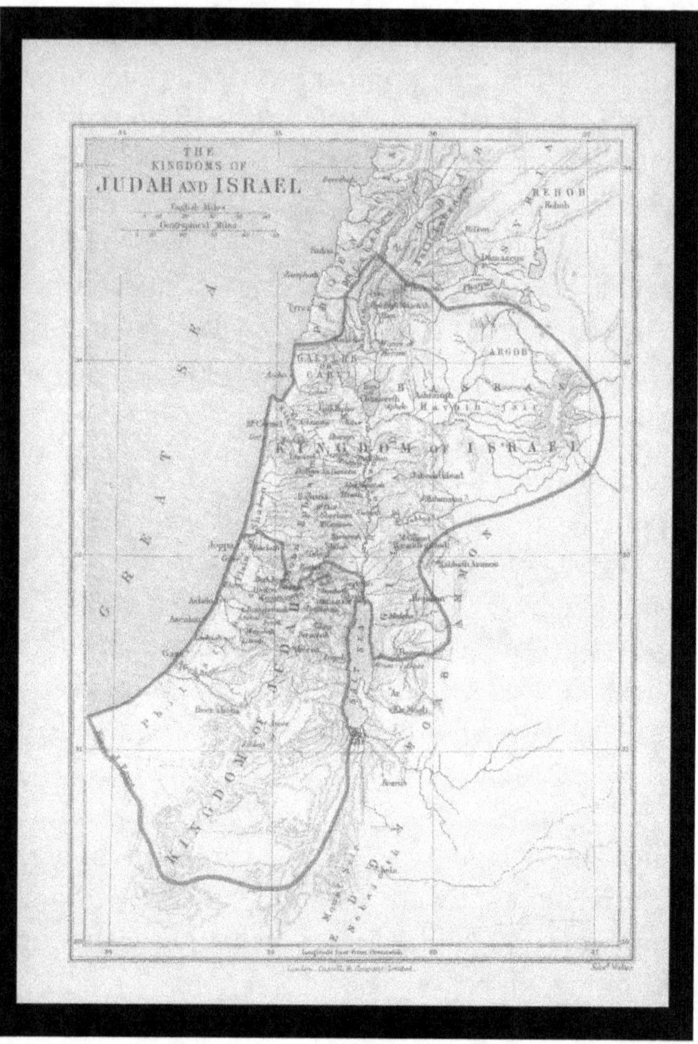

(Kingdoms of Judah and Israel): (Edward Weller,
The Kingdoms of Judah and Israel, Public Domain)

In the north, the Kingdom of Israel faced challenges from both internal factions and external enemies. The Omride dynasty, established by King Omri in the early 9th century BC, marked a period of relative stability and expansion. Omri's successors, including his son Ahab, strengthened Israel's political and economic ties with neighboring states through strategic marriages and alliances. However, the northern kingdom's prosperity was undermined by religious and social tensions. The introduction of foreign deities and the worship of Baal, encouraged by Ahab's marriage to the Phoenician princess Jezebel, led to conflicts with the Yahweh-focused prophetic movement. The biblical accounts of the prophets Elijah and Elisha highlight the religious and social turmoil that characterized this period.

In contrast, the southern Kingdom of Judah maintained a more stable dynastic line, centered around the Davidic lineage. The religious significance of Jerusalem and the Temple helped solidify Judah's identity and political cohesion. However, Judah was not immune to external threats. It faced incursions from neighboring states and periodic subjugation by larger empires.

The period of the divided kingdoms witnessed significant religious developments and the emergence of prophetic figures who played crucial roles in shaping Israelite society. The prophets, often seen as intermediaries between God and the people, challenged political authorities. They called for social justice and warned of impending divine judgment.

In the northern kingdom, prophets such as Elijah and Elisha became prominent figures, advocating the worship of Yahweh and denouncing the influence of foreign deities. Their dramatic confrontations with the royal family and the priests of Baal underscored the deep religious divisions within Israelite society. In Judah, the prophets Isaiah and Micah emerged as influential voices, addressing issues of social justice, covenantal faithfulness, and the threat of foreign invasion. Isaiah, in particular, offered a theological perspective that emphasized the centrality of Jerusalem and the Davidic dynasty in God's plan for Israel. The prophetic movement played a vital role in shaping the religious and ethical ideals of the Israelite community. Their messages, often recorded and preserved in written form, laid the foundation for the development of Hebrew scripture and contributed to the evolution of monotheism.

However, the prosperity of the Kingdom of Israel did not last. As early as the 9th century BC, the Israelites came into conflict with the **Assyrians**. These were their easterly neighbors who were steadily expanding their realm and soon became the dominant force in the Levant. The Assyrian kings, such as Tiglath-Pileser III and Sargon II, embarked on campaigns of expansion that brought them into direct conflict with the Israelite kingdoms. The Kingdom of Israel, with its strategic location along key trade routes, became a target of Assyrian aggression. In response to Assyrian pressure, Israel often sought alliances with other regional powers, such as Aram-Damascus and Egypt. However, these alliances proved insufficient to withstand the military might of the Assyrians.

According to the surviving Assyrian records, most notably the Kurkh Monoliths, an alliance was made in 854 BC between Ahab of Israel and Ben-Hadad II of the Kingdom of Aram-Damascus. In the same year, they came to blows with the Assyrians and managed to halt their sudden expansion with a victory at the Battle of Qarqar. But this victory brought only short-lived respite. In 722 BC, the Assyrian king Shalmaneser V launched a campaign against Israel, culminating in the capture of their capital Samaria and the destruction of the northern kingdom. The fall of Israel resulted in the exodus of a significant portion of its population, described in the Bible as the "Lost Tribes of Israel." The Assyrians implemented a policy of mass deportation and resettlement, aiming to prevent further rebellion and integrate the region into their empire. There is no doubt that the destruction of the northern kingdom marked a turning point in the history of the Israelites. Many of its people fled south to seek refuge in Judah. The loss of the northern kingdom also reinforced Judah's status as the sole remaining Israelite state, further solidifying Jerusalem's importance as a religious and political center.

The southern Kingdom of Judah, while initially spared from Assyrian conquest, faced its own set of challenges during this period. The Assyrian threat forced Judah to navigate a delicate balance between paying tribute to Assyria and maintaining its autonomy. The biblical accounts of kings such as Hezekiah highlight Judah's efforts to resist Assyrian domination through religious reforms and fortifications. Hezekiah's reign, from 715 to 686 BC, is notable for his attempts to strengthen Judah's defenses and assert its independence. The construction of the Siloam Tunnel and the expansion of Jerusalem's walls reflect Hezekiah's focus on fortifying the city against potential sieges. His religious reforms, aimed at centralizing worship in Jerusalem and eliminating pagan practices, are depicted in the Bible as efforts to align Judah more closely with Yahweh's covenant.

Despite these efforts, Judah's relationship with Assyria remained fraught with tension. In 701 BC, the Assyrian king Sennacherib launched a campaign against Judah, capturing numerous fortified cities and besieging Jerusalem. The biblical narrative describes a miraculous deliverance of Jerusalem. It was attributed to divine intervention, but the archaeological evidence suggests a more complex series of events, including the payment of tribute to secure Assyrian withdrawal.

The period of the divided kingdoms witnessed significant cultural and religious developments that shaped the identity of the Israelite people. The experiences of conquest, exile, and religious reform contributed to the evolution of religious practices and beliefs. This laid the groundwork for the emergence of a distinct Israelite identity.

The Wrath of Babylon

We now understand that the southern Kingdom of Judah managed to endure longer than its northern counterpart. This was thanks, in part, to its more stable dynastic line and its strategic location. However, Judah's eventual downfall was precipitated by a combination of internal weaknesses and the relentless expansion of powerful empires in the region, particularly the Babylonian Empire.

In the late 7th century BC, the Assyrian Empire, which had dominated the Near East for centuries, began to weaken due to internal strife and external pressures. This decline gave rise to the Neo-Babylonian Empire, led by King Nabopolassar and his son Nebuchadnezzar II, who seized the opportunity to expand their influence. The Babylonians quickly established themselves as the new superpower in the region, capturing vast territories previously under Assyrian control. Judah, which had been a vassal state under Assyrian rule, found itself in a precarious position as the balance of power shifted. King Josiah of Judah, who reigned from 640 to 609 BC, attempted to capitalize on Assyria's decline. He asserted greater independence and initiated significant religious reforms. These reforms aimed to purify Judah's religious practices by centralizing worship in Jerusalem and eliminating foreign influences. They are recorded in the biblical account of Josiah's discovery of the "Book of the Law" during Temple renovations. However, Josiah's ambitious plans were cut short when he was killed in battle at Megiddo in 609 BC. He had been trying to intercept the Egyptian Pharaoh Necho II, who was marching north to support the Assyrians against the Babylonians. Josiah's death left a power vacuum that would prove destabilizing for Judah.

Josiah was succeeded by several weak kings who struggled to maintain control. His son Jehoahaz ascended to the throne, but he was quickly deposed by Pharaoh Necho II and replaced by his brother Jehoiakim, who reigned as a vassal of Egypt. The shifting alliances and Judah's precarious position between the competing powers of Egypt and Babylon made the kingdom vulnerable. Jehoiakim's reign (609–598 BC) was marked by tensions with Babylon. He initially aligned with Egypt but later switched allegiance to Babylon under Nebuchadnezzar II. However, when Egypt failed to counter Babylon's rising power, Jehoiakim rebelled against Babylonian rule, provoking Nebuchadnezzar's ire.

In 597 BC, Nebuchadnezzar besieged Jerusalem in response to Jehoiakim's revolt. Jehoiakim died during the siege, and his son Jehoiachin surrendered to the Babylonians, leading to his deportation, along with other prominent citizens of Jerusalem. Nebuchadnezzar installed Zedekiah, another son of Josiah, as a puppet king.

Zedekiah's reign (597–586 BC) was marked by increasing tension with Babylon. Encouraged by Egyptian promises of support and the unrest among Babylon's subject states, Zedekiah eventually rebelled against Nebuchadnezzar. This decision had catastrophic consequences for Judah. In 589 BCE, Nebuchadnezzar launched a final campaign against Jerusalem. The Babylonian army besieged the city, cutting off supplies and weakening its defenses over an extended period. The biblical accounts and archaeological evidence describe a grim scene as the inhabitants of Jerusalem faced starvation and disease during the prolonged siege. In 586 BC, after a siege lasting over a year and a half, the Babylonians breached Jerusalem's walls. The city was sacked, and the First Temple was destroyed, marking the end of the Kingdom of Judah.

The destruction of the Temple was a devastating blow to the Israelites, as it represented the loss of their foremost spiritual and cultural center. Nebuchadnezzar's forces captured King Zedekiah, blinded him, and took him in chains to Babylon, along with many of Judah's leaders and skilled artisans. This event, known as the Babylonian Exile, saw a significant portion of the population deported to Babylon, while those who remained faced harsh conditions under Babylonian rule.

In Babylon, the exiled Israelites faced the challenge of maintaining their distinct religious and cultural identity in a foreign land. The exile became a time of significant religious development. There was an increased emphasis on prayer, study, and the observance of religious laws, conducted mostly in secrecy in their homes. This period saw the beginnings of the Jewish diaspora, as communities of Jews settled in various parts of the Babylonian Empire and beyond.

The Babylonian Exile also contributed to the development of Jewish scripture and literature, as the exiled community sought to preserve their traditions and teachings through written texts. This period of reflection and adaptation laid the groundwork for the eventual compilation of the Hebrew Bible, which would become central to Jewish religious life.

The fall of Jerusalem and the Babylonian Exile had profound theological and cultural implications for the Israelites. The loss of the First Temple and the deportation to Babylon forced the Jewish people to re-evaluate their identity and relationship with God. The prophetic writings of this period, particularly those of Jeremiah and Ezekiel, reflect the deep sense of loss and the search for meaning in the face of disaster. Theological reflections during the exile emphasized themes of repentance, renewal, and the hope of eventual restoration. The destruction of the Temple was interpreted as a divine punishment for the people's unfaithfulness to the covenant. But prophets such as Isaiah and Ezekiel also offered a vision of future redemption, when the covenant would be renewed and the Temple rebuilt. This hope was realized in 539 BC when the rising Persian king Cyrus the Great conquered Babylon. He then issued a decree allowing the exiled peoples, including the Jews, to return to their homelands and rebuild their temples. The return from exile marked a new chapter in the history of Israel, leading to the reconstruction of the Temple and the establishment of the Second Temple period.

Chapter 3
The Hellenistic and Roman Eras
in Ancient Israel

In 334 BC, Alexander the Great embarked on his legendary campaign against the Persian Empire. He rapidly conquered vast territories across Asia Minor, the Levant, Egypt, and beyond. By 332 BC, Alexander had successfully taken control of the Levant, including the region of Judea, which had been under Persian rule. His conquests brought significant changes to the region. These included the introduction of Greek (Hellenistic) administration, the establishment of new cities, and the promotion of the Greek language and culture. Alexander's approach to governance was unique in that he sought to blend Greek and local customs, a policy often referred to as "Hellenization." In Judea, this policy meant that Greek culture began to permeate Jewish society, affecting language, art, education, and religious practices. The establishment of new cities, such as Alexandria in Egypt, served as hubs of Greek culture and

attracted a diverse population of Greeks, Jews, and other ethnic groups.

While Alexander himself did not interfere directly with Jewish religious practices, the presence of Greek culture posed a challenge to traditional Jewish life. The Jewish community in Judea found itself navigating a complex cultural landscape, where Greek philosophy, art, and governance coexisted with Jewish religious traditions and practices. Following Alexander's death in 323 BC, his vast empire was divided among his generals, known as the Diadochi, leading to the emergence of several Hellenistic kingdoms.

(Marble Head of Alexander the Great, Beth Shean, Public Domain)

The two most relevant to the Jewish experience were the Ptolemaic Kingdom, based in Egypt, and the Seleucid Empire, which controlled much of the former Persian territories in Asia, including Syria and Mesopotamia. Initially, Judea came under the control of the Ptolemaic dynasty, which ruled from Alexandria. The Ptolemies generally adopted a pragmatic approach to governance, allowing the Jews a degree of religious autonomy while encouraging the adoption of Greek culture. The Jewish community in Alexandria, one of the largest outside of Judea, became a significant center of Jewish life and intellectual activity. The period of Ptolemaic rule was marked by economic growth and cultural exchange. The Jews in Alexandria engaged with Greek philosophy and literature, leading to the production of works that sought to harmonize Greek and Jewish thought. The most famous of these works is the "Septuagint," a Greek translation of the Hebrew Bible, which became an essential text for the Jewish diaspora.

However, in the early 2nd century BC, control of Judea shifted from the Ptolemies to the Seleucid Empire. This transition marked the beginning of a more tumultuous period for the Jewish people, as the Seleucid rulers adopted increasingly aggressive policies of Hellenization. Antiochus III, also known as Antiochus the Great, initially maintained a policy of relative tolerance toward Jewish practices. However, his successors, particularly Antiochus IV Epiphanes, pursued a more aggressive program of cultural assimilation. Antiochus IV's reign (175–164 BC) was characterized by efforts to unify his empire through the imposition of Greek culture and religion. He sought to transform Jerusalem into a Hellenistic city, establishing Greek institutions and promoting Greek religious practices. The construction of a gymnasium and the introduction of Greek athletic contests were emblematic of this cultural shift. They represented a direct challenge to traditional Jewish values and customs.

Tensions between the Hellenizing policies of the Seleucid rulers and the traditional Jewish community came to a head in 167 BC when Antiochus IV issued decrees prohibiting Jewish religious practices, including circumcision and Sabbath observance. The most provocative act was the desecration of the Second Temple in Jerusalem, where an altar to Zeus was erected and pigs were sacrificed. This blatant violation of Jewish sacred space and practices was the major catalyst for the Maccabean Revolt. The revolt was led by the Hasmonean family, commonly known as the Maccabees. It began in 167 BC, when Mattathias, a Jewish priest from the town of Modiin, refused to comply with the king's orders to perform pagan sacrifices and killed a Hellenistic official. Mattathias and his sons, John Gaddi, Simon Thassi, Judas Maccabeus, Eleazar Avaran, and Jonathan Apphus, subsequently fled to the Judean hills, where they organized a guerrilla campaign against the Seleucid forces.

The Maccabean Revolt

The Maccabean Revolt was a pivotal moment in Jewish history; it represented a determined resistance against cultural assimilation and religious persecution. Judas Maccabeus, known as "The Hammer," emerged as a charismatic leader, rallying the Jewish population and achieving a series of military victories against the Seleucids. The Maccabean Revolt is notable for its strategic military campaigns and key battles that showcased the tactical brilliance of Judas Maccabeus and his forces. The early successes of the Maccabees were marked by their ability to conduct surprise attacks and use unconventional tactics. These factors compensated for their lack of resources and manpower compared to the well-equipped Seleucid armies.

One of the first major victories for the Maccabees was the Battle of Wadi Haramia (also known as the Battle of the Ascent of Lebonah) fought in 166 BC.

In this encounter, Judas and his forces ambushed a Seleucid convoy, capturing weapons and supplies. This victory was crucial in building the confidence of the Maccabean forces and attracting more recruits to their cause. Another significant battle was fought at Beth Horon, where the Maccabees used the narrow and steep terrain to their advantage, defeating a larger Seleucid force led by General Seron. Perhaps the most famous battle of the revolt, however, was the Battle of Emmaus, fought in 165 BC. In this engagement, Judas Maccabeus demonstrated his strategic acumen by deceiving the Seleucid commanders, Gorgias and Nicanor. While the Seleucid forces were lured into a false sense of security, expecting an easy victory, Judas launched a surprise attack on their camp, leading to a decisive Maccabean victory. The success at Emmaus solidified Judas's reputation as a formidable military leader and further galvanized the Jewish resistance.

The Maccabean Revolt also saw the effective use of guerrilla warfare, which involved hit-and-run attacks, ambushes, and sabotage. The Maccabees avoided direct confrontations with the larger and more powerful Seleucid armies, instead focusing on disrupting their supply lines and communication networks. This approach not only weakened the Seleucid forces but also allowed the Maccabees to conserve their resources and maintain their mobility.

One of the most significant outcomes of the Maccabean Revolt was the restoration of the Second Temple in Jerusalem, an event that holds great religious and cultural significance for Jews worldwide. After a series of successful military campaigns, Judas Maccabeus and his forces recaptured Jerusalem in 164 BC.

(Judas Maccabeus, Woodcut by Julius Schnorr von Carolsfeld (1794–1872)) (Schnorr von Carolsfeld, Bibel in Bildern, 1860, Public Domain)

Upon entering the city, they found the Temple desecrated and in disrepair, with pagan idols and altars defiling its sacred space. The Maccabees immediately set about purifying and rededicating the Temple. They removed the pagan symbols, cleansed the altar, and resumed the traditional Jewish rituals that had been suppressed under Seleucid rule. This restoration culminated in the celebration of Hanukkah, a festival commemorating the rededication of the Temple and the miracle of the oil. According to Jewish tradition, the Maccabees found only a small amount of oil sufficient to light the menorah for one day, yet it miraculously burned for eight days. Hanukkah, also known as the Festival of Lights, is celebrated annually by Jews around the world to this day. The restoration of the Temple was not only a religious triumph but also a powerful symbol of Jewish resilience and determination. It marked the re-establishment of Jewish religious practices and the reaffirmation of their cultural identity in the face of external pressures. The success of the Maccabean Revolt and the restoration of the Temple had a profound impact on Jewish consciousness, reinforcing the themes of resistance, faith, and divine intervention that resonate in Jewish history.

The success of the Maccabean Revolt led to the establishment of the Hasmonean dynasty, which ruled Judea as an independent kingdom for nearly a century. Under the Hasmoneans, Judea experienced a period of relative autonomy and prosperity, although internal divisions and external pressures continued to pose challenges.

Ultimately, the Hellenistic period was characterized by a complex cultural synthesis that left a lasting impact on Jewish society. While the Maccabean Revolt represented a reaction against forced Hellenization, it did not entirely reverse the influence of Greek culture on Jewish life. Instead, a more nuanced cultural synthesis occurred, as elements of Greek and Jewish traditions merged. One significant aspect of this synthesis was the development of Jewish-Greek literature and philosophy. Jewish scholars in the Hellenistic world engaged with Greek philosophical thought, producing works that sought to reconcile Jewish teachings with Greek philosophy. Notable examples include the writings of Philo of Alexandria, a Jewish philosopher who sought to harmonize Jewish theology with Platonic philosophy and the *Book of Wisdom*. This work reflects Hellenistic influences in its language and themes. The influence of Greek language and thought also extended to the Jewish diaspora communities, particularly in Egypt and Asia Minor.

The use of Greek as a *lingua franca* facilitated the spread of Jewish ideas and practices across the Hellenistic world, allowing for greater interaction and exchange between Jewish and non-Jewish communities. The Hellenistic period also witnessed the emergence of new Jewish sects and movements, reflecting the diverse responses to the challenges and opportunities presented by Greek culture. The Pharisees, Sadducees, and Essenes were among the prominent Jewish groups that developed during this time. Each one had its distinct interpretation of Jewish law and tradition.

The Hellenistic period was a time of profound transformation and adaptation for the Jewish people. The encounter with Greek culture and the challenges posed by foreign rule forced Jewish society to grapple with questions of identity, religious practice, and cultural assimilation. This era laid the groundwork for the development of Judaism as a distinct and resilient religious tradition, capable of adapting to changing historical circumstances. The experiences of the Hellenistic period also set the stage for the later encounters between Judaism and other world cultures. These included Roman, Christian, and Islamic civilizations. The cultural synthesis that emerged during this time demonstrated the capacity of Jewish tradition to engage with and incorporate elements of surrounding cultures, all the while maintaining its core beliefs and practices.

There was, however, a wholly new power arising on the global stage. Following the dominion of Alexander the Great, a fledgling kingdom was gradually increasing its presence. The city-state of **Rome**, always hungry for more land and power, expanded steadily across Europe, the Middle East, and the Mediterranean, consuming its neighboring cities and tribes. Rome soon evolved into a highly advanced civilization, a Republic that became a major player in global events. By the time it came into contact with the Jewish people in what is today Israel, the Roman Republic was at the height of its power, with influential figures such as Julius Caesar and Pompey the Great dominating the political and social scene.

In the mid-1st century BC, Judea was a semi-independent realm within the Seleucid Empire, ruled by the Hasmonean Dynasty established by the close descendants of Judas Maccabeus. However, as the Seleucid Empire slowly declined, a dynastic dispute arose between Hyrcanus II and Aristobulus II over control of the Jewish state. The subsequent

Hasmonean Civil War gave Rome an opportunity to become involved, and in 63 BC, the Roman general Pompey conquered Jerusalem. Judea became a client state under Roman oversight, marking the start of the Republic's domination in the region. Although Hyrcanus II was installed as a high priest and ethnarch, the real power was concentrated in the hands of the Romans and their appointed administrators.

The loss of political autonomy came as a major blow to Jewish pride and self-determination. The authorities in Rome were quick to impose taxes, reorganize the structure of governances, and station their own troops in the region. However, the Romans still allowed a degree of religious autonomy, as they understood the centrality of the Second Temple and the Jewish law to the identity of the Jewish people.

The most notable figure during the early Roman period in Israel was Herod the Great, who ruled the region and province of Judea from 37 BC until his death in 4 BC – a total of 33 years. Herod was a complex and controversial figure. His reign exemplified the tensions between the Jewish traditions and the imperial power of Rome. He was born to a father from Idumea (Edom) and a mother from Nabatea (an Arab nation), so his lineage and his close alliance with Rome made him a somewhat unpopular figure among the Jewish populace.

Herod secured his position as the King of Judea with the backing of Rome, particularly under the favor of Mark Antony and, later, Octavian Augustus. His reign was marked by a series of ambitious and almost megalomaniac building projects, which included a massive expansion of the Second Temple in Jerusalem. It subsequently became one of the most magnificent structures of the ancient world. Some other construction projects he completed were the port city of Caesarea Maritima, the massive fortress at Masada, and the Herodium, a palace-fortress near Bethlehem. Yet despite these grand achievements, Herod's rule was characterized by a degree of paranoia and brutality. Always wary and suspicious, he did not shy from removing those he deemed a threat to his rule. He executed several members of his own family, including his wife Mariamne and her sons for fear they might challenge his authority. Besides this, his reign was marked by heavy taxation and forced labor, which, combined with his perceived favoritism towards Rome, alienated many of his Jewish subjects.

But Herod could not reign forever. In his later years, he suffered from a major illness and died in 4

BC. His vast kingdom was divided among his sons, which led, as was often the case, to more instability. Eventually, Judea came under direct Roman administration as one of its many provinces. It was controlled by a series of Roman governors, known as procurators. This period was marked by increasing tensions between the Jewish population and the authorities of Rome, which set the stage for future conflict.

(Image: Pompey the Great, Public Domain)

During the early Roman period, Jewish society was marked by significant religious and social diversity. The most prominent groups were the Pharisees, Sadducees, Essenes, and Zealots. The Pharisees emphasized the importance of oral tradition and the interpretation of their holy book, the Torah. They believed in the resurrection of the dead and the existence of angels, which set them apart from the more conservative Sadducees, who focused on the literal text of the Torah. Their power was centered in the Temple, making them more aligned with the aristocratic and priestly classes. The Essenes were a smaller, more ascetic sect that withdrew from mainstream society to form monastic communities. Of these, the most famous was at Qumran, near the Dead Sea. The Essenes emphasized purity, communal living, and a strict interpretation of Jewish law. The discovery of the Dead Sea Scrolls in the mid-20th century provided invaluable insights into their beliefs and practices. The Zealots were a radical and nationalist movement that emerged in response to Roman occupation. They rejected Roman rule and advocated armed resistance, believing that Jewish independence could be achieved only through violent uprising. The Zealots played a crucial role in the First Jewish Revolt against Rome, which ultimately led to the destruction of the Second Temple.

The First Jewish Revolt and the Destruction of the Second Temple

The First Jewish Revolt (66 to 70 AD) was a watershed moment in Jewish history, marking the culmination of growing discontent with Roman rule. The revolt was sparked by a combination of factors, including heavy taxation, religious tensions, and Roman disrespect for Jewish customs and the Temple. The immediate catalyst was the actions of the Roman governor Gessius Florus, whose oppressive policies and looting of the Temple treasury incited widespread anger. The revolt quickly spread throughout Judea, with Jewish forces achieving several early victories against the Romans. However, the Roman response was overwhelming. The emperor Nero appointed Vespasian, a skilled general, to suppress the rebellion. Vespasian, along with his son Titus, systematically recaptured Jewish territory, culminating in the siege of Jerusalem in 70 AD.

The siege of Jerusalem was brutal and devastating. The city's defenders were divided by internal strife, with different factions fighting not only against the Romans but also against each other. As the Romans breached the city's defenses, they set fire to the Temple, reducing it to ruins. The destruction of the Second Temple was a catastrophic event for the Jewish people, symbolizing the loss of their spiritual and national center. It marked the end of the Second Temple period. Many Jews were killed, enslaved, or forced to flee, leading to a significant diaspora. The destruction also had a lasting impact on Jewish religious practice, as the focus of worship shifted from the Temple to the synagogue and the study of the Torah.

Following the fall of Jerusalem, a subgroup of the Zealots, known as the Sicarii, fled to Masada under the leadership of Eleazar ben Ya'ir. Their name, derived from the Latin word *sica*, meaning dagger, translates as "knife-wielders" or "dagger-wielders." They carried small concealed daggers and would assassinate Romans and Jewish collaborators swiftly and covertly in public places, before disappearing into the crowds. They resorted to various acts of terrorism to incite the Jewish people to war against the Romans.

Image: (Aerial view of Masada, Andrew Shiva)

Eleazar ben Ya'ir was a descendant of Judas of Galilee, a prominent Jewish leader who had led a revolt against the Roman census in 6 AD. Eleazar inherited his forefather's militant resistance to Roman rule and became a key figure in the Jewish rebellion. He was a charismatic and determined leader who inspired his followers to continue their fight for freedom, even in the face of overwhelming odds. Eleazar's leadership at Masada was marked by his unwavering commitment to Jewish independence and his refusal to submit to Roman authority. The Sicarii were joined at Masada by other refugees, including women and children, swelling their numbers to around 960. The decision to retreat to Masada after the fall of Jerusalem was a calculated move to continue the resistance from a defensible position.

Masada is a natural fortress located on a plateau overlooking the Judean Desert and the Dead Sea. It was originally fortified by Hasmonean rulers and expanded in the first century BC by Herod the Great, who constructed two opulent palaces, storerooms, cisterns, and barracks on the summit. The fortress was a marvel of engineering, with water supply systems capable of sustaining long sieges. Its remote location and steep sides made it nearly impregnable to conventional assault.

The Roman campaign to subdue Masada began in 72 AD. The Roman governor of Judea, Lucius Flavius Silva, was tasked with eliminating the last pockets of resistance, and Masada was the final target. Silva marched his troops, the Roman Tenth Legion (Legio X Fretensis), along with auxiliary forces and Jewish slaves, to the base of the fortress. Recognizing that a frontal assault on Masada was nearly impossible due to its location, the Romans employed a siege strategy. They built a series of camps around the fortress, cutting off the defenders from the outside world. The most famous element of the Roman siege was the construction of a massive ramp on the western side of the plateau. Using Jewish slaves, the Romans gradually built the ramp from earth and stones, eventually creating a path that allowed their siege engines to reach the fortress walls. The construction of the ramp was an extraordinary feat of engineering. It was more than 100 meters (330 feet) high and took months to complete. During this time, the defenders of Masada could do little to stop the Romans, as their position on the top of the cliffs made it difficult to launch counterattacks. As the ramp neared completion, Eleazar ben Ya'ir and his followers realized that the fall of Masada was inevitable.

As the Roman forces prepared to breach the walls of Masada, Eleazar ben Ya'ir faced a terrible dilemma. Surrendering to the Romans would mean slavery or death for his followers, as the Romans were unlikely to show mercy to the Sicarii, whom they considered terrorists. Moreover, Roman conquest would result in the desecration of Jewish religious traditions and the destruction of their community's autonomy. In the face of these grim prospects, Eleazar made a fateful decision. He addressed his followers in a stirring speech, urging them to choose death over enslavement. According to the Romano-Jewish historian Flavius Josephus, who provides the only surviving account of the siege, Eleazar's speech emphasized the ideals of freedom and martyrdom. He argued that it was better to die by their own hands than to submit to the Romans and endure the humiliation of slavery. The speech which Josephus wrote down is likely fictional but nevertheless inspired many generations of Jewish people. According to him, Eleazar urged his followers, "Let us die unenslaved by our enemies, and leave this world as free men, in company with our wives and children."

The community at Masada agreed to this course of action. Eleazar and his followers organized a mass suicide, whereby each man killed his own family members, and then they cast lots to determine who would kill the remaining men. In the end, the last survivor was tasked with taking his own life. When the Romans breached the walls of Masada the following morning, they were met with silence. As they entered the fortress, they discovered the bodies of the defenders – men, women, and children – who had chosen death over captivity. According to Josephus, two women and five children had hidden in a cistern and survived the massacre, later telling the Romans what had happened. The fall of Masada marked the end of the First Jewish-Roman War. Roman control over Judea was re-established, and the province remained under Roman rule for several centuries.

Still, the revolt at Masada and the mass suicide led by Eleazar ben Ya'ir have been subjects of intense historical and cultural debate. The primary source for these events is the work of Flavius Josephus; his account in his book *The Jewish War* is the only contemporary description of the siege. While Josephus' work provides invaluable information, it has been scrutinized for its biases, as Josephus was writing for a Roman audience and may have exaggerated or embellished certain aspects of the story.

For centuries, the events at Masada were largely forgotten, but in modern times, they have been revived as a potent symbol of Jewish resistance and national identity. In the 20th century, Masada became a focal point for Zionist movements and the newly founded state of Israel. The phrase "Masada shall not fall again" became a rallying cry, symbolizing the determination to defend Jewish autonomy and sovereignty.

Masada is now a UNESCO World Heritage Site and a popular destination for tourists and scholars. Archaeological excavations in the 1960s, led by

Yigael Yadin, uncovered significant remains of the fortress, including Herod's palaces, Roman siege works, and the synagogue used by the defenders. These findings have helped to corroborate parts of Josephus' account, though the mass suicide has remained a topic of debate among historians.

In the aftermath of the First Jewish Revolt, the Romans established a new city, Aelia Capitolina, on the ruins of Jerusalem. The Temple Mount was desecrated, and a Roman temple to Jupiter was erected on the site of the destroyed Second Temple. Despite the devastation, Jewish resistance to Roman rule persisted. The most significant uprising after the First Jewish Revolt was the Bar Kokhba Revolt (132 to 136 AD). Led by Simon Bar Kokhba, who was regarded by some as the Messiah, this revolt sought to re-establish Jewish independence and rebuild the Temple. Bar Kokhba's forces initially achieved some successes, and for a brief period, an independent Jewish state was re-established.

However, the Roman response was once again decisive and brutal. The emperor Hadrian dispatched a large military force to crush the rebellion. The Roman legions methodically besieged and destroyed the Jewish strongholds, and Bar Kokhba himself was killed in battle. The revolt was crushed, and the consequences were severe. Hadrian enacted harsh measures to suppress Jewish identity and practice, including a ban on circumcision and the renaming of Judea as Syria Palaestina to erase the connection between the land and the Jewish people.

This era saw the rise of Rabbinic Judaism, which emerged as a response to the challenges posed by the loss of the Temple and the dispersal of the Jewish population.

Thus we see that the Roman period in Israel's ancient history was a time of profound change and upheaval. The Jewish people faced the loss of political sovereignty, the destruction of their most sacred institution, and the challenge of maintaining their identity in the face of foreign rule. Yet, despite these challenges, the Roman period also witnessed the resilience and adaptability of Jewish society. The destruction of the Second Temple and the suppression of the Bar Kokhba Revolt marked the end of ancient Jewish statehood, but they also set the stage for the development of Rabbinic Judaism. This new teaching would preserve and transmit Jewish traditions through the centuries. The period also saw the emergence of early Christianity, which would go on to become a major world religion, deeply intertwined with the history of the land of

Israel. Undoubtedly, this period left a lasting legacy on the land and its people. The events of this era are still remembered and commemorated in Jewish religious practice, and the archaeological remains from this time continue to be a source of fascination and study. The Roman period was a time of great loss, but it was also a time of renewal and transformation, shaping the course of Jewish history and identity for generations to come.

Chapter 4
The Jewish Diaspora
and the Rise of Rabbinic Judaism

The fall of Jerusalem and the destruction of the Second Temple by the Romans in 70 AD decisively shattered the last vestiges of Jewish sovereignty in the land of Israel. The loss of the Temple, the epicenter of Jewish religious and communal life, left a profound void in Jewish society. The immediate aftermath of this catastrophe saw the beginning of a mass dispersion of the Jewish people across the Roman Empire and beyond. Shaken and uprooted, these people sought a new beginning elsewhere, beyond the borders of their homeland and far within the Roman Empire. This process intensified following the Bar Kokhba Revolt (132 to 136 AD). The diaspora was not a new phenomenon in Jewish history. Jewish communities had existed outside the land of Israel since the Babylonian Exile in the 6th century BC, a similar expulsion episode, and during the Hellenistic period, significant Jewish populations were established in places such as

Alexandria in Egypt and Antioch in Syria. However, the destruction of the Second Temple and the notorious wrath of Rome accelerated this process, leading to a more widespread and permanent dispersal of the Jewish people.

In the wake of the Temple's destruction, Jews were forcibly exiled from Jerusalem, with many sold into slavery or executed, which often happened in lands oppressed by Rome. Those who survived scattered across the Mediterranean basin, settling in regions such as North Africa, Asia Minor, Greece, Italy, and farther afield in Europe and the Middle East.

(Students of Talmud, by Ephraim Moses Linen)
(Image: The Talmud Students, Public Domain)

These dispersed communities, though geographically distant from one another, maintained their Jewish identity through shared religious practices, communal structures, and the preservation of Hebrew as a liturgical language. However, the dispersion had profound consequences for Jewish identity and religious life. No longer could the Jewish people rely on the central authority of the Temple or the priesthood. Instead, they had to adapt to a new reality in which their religious and communal life would be sustained under foreign rule and often in the face of varying degrees of hostility or tolerance from their host societies.

It was in this context that Rabbinic Judaism emerged from the teachings and traditions of the Pharisees, a Jewish sect that had flourished during the Second Temple period. Unlike the Sadducees, who were closely tied to the Temple and its rituals, the Pharisees emphasized the study of the Torah, oral traditions, and the application of Jewish law (*halakhah*) to everyday life. This emphasis on legal interpretation and ethical behavior became the foundation of Rabbinic Judaism. The rabbis, who were scholars and teachers of Jewish law, became the new religious authorities in the post-Temple world. They developed a system of study and interpretation that allowed for the continued observance of Jewish law even without the Temple.

Central to this system was the Oral Torah, a body of traditions and interpretations that were believed to have been handed down alongside the written Torah (the first five books of the Hebrew Bible). The Oral Torah provided the rabbis with the flexibility to adapt Jewish law to new circumstances while remaining faithful to the covenant between God and the Jewish people.

The early rabbinic period saw the establishment of key centers of learning, particularly in Jabneh (Yavneh), a town in Judea where the Sanhedrin, the supreme Jewish legal and religious council, was reconstituted after the destruction of the Temple. Under the leadership of figures such as Rabbi Yochanan ben Zakkai (fl. 1st c. AD), Jabneh became a hub of rabbinic scholarship and a symbol of Jewish resilience. It was here that the foundations of Rabbinic Judaism were laid, including the codification of prayer, the establishment of the synagogue as a central institution, and the development of new rituals to replace the Temple service. The synagogues, which had existed in various forms before the destruction of the Temple, now became the focal points of Jewish communal life. In these houses of worship, study, and assembly, Jews could gather to pray, read from the Torah, and engage in communal decision-making. The synagogue also served as a place of education, where Jewish children and adults alike could learn the teachings of the Torah and the traditions of their ancestors.

The Compiling of the Mishnah and the Talmud

One of the most significant achievements of the early rabbinic period was the compilation of the Mishnah, the first major written collection of Jewish oral traditions. The Mishnah was compiled around 200 AD by Rabbi Judah the Prince (*Yehuda HaNasi*) and his colleagues. It represented a monumental effort to preserve and systematize the vast body of oral law that had been transmitted orally for generations. The Mishnah is organized into six orders (*sedarim*), each dealing with a different aspect of Jewish life: *Zeraim* (agriculture and prayer), *Moed* (festivals and Sabbath), *Nashim* (marriage and divorce), *Nezikin* (civil and criminal law), *Kodashim* (Temple service and sacrifices), and *Tohorot* (purity laws). Within these orders, the Mishnah is further divided into tractates, chapters, and individual teachings (*mishnayot*).

The decision to write down the oral traditions was motivated by several factors. The dispersion of the

Jewish people and the decline of traditional centers of learning raised concerns that the oral law might be forgotten or distorted over time. By committing the oral traditions to writing, the rabbis sought to ensure the preservation and continuity of Jewish law and practice.

The Mishnah also reflects the diversity of Jewish thought during this period. It includes the opinions and interpretations of different rabbis, often presenting multiple viewpoints on a given issue. This pluralism is a hallmark of Rabbinic Judaism, which values debate and discussion as means of arriving at legal and ethical decisions. The Mishnah does not always provide definitive answers but instead offers a framework within which Jewish law can be applied and interpreted in different contexts.

The compilation of the Mishnah had a profound impact on Jewish life. It became the foundational text of Rabbinic Judaism, studied and debated by generations of rabbis and scholars. The Mishnah also served as the basis for the development of the Talmud, a much larger and more complex work that would come to play a central role in Jewish life and thought.

Following the completion of the Mishnah, rabbinic scholarship entered a new phase marked by the development of the Talmud. The Talmud is a comprehensive collection of rabbinic discussions, interpretations, and commentaries on the Mishnah, as well as on various aspects of Jewish law, ethics, and theology. The Talmud is not a single work but rather consists of two versions: the Jerusalem Talmud (*Talmud Yerushalmi*) and the Babylonian Talmud (*Talmud Bavli*). The Jerusalem Talmud was compiled in the land of Israel during the 4th and 5th centuries AD. It reflects the teachings and discussions of the rabbis (*amoraim*) who lived and studied in the academies of Tiberias, Sepphoris, and other centers of Jewish life in the region. The Jerusalem Talmud is shorter and less comprehensive than its Babylonian counterpart, and its language (a mix of Hebrew and Aramaic) is more difficult for later generations to understand.

(Image: Carl Schleicher, Jüdische Szene 1, Public Domain)

The Babylonian Talmud, on the other hand, was compiled over several centuries in the Jewish academies of Babylonia (modern-day Iraq), reaching its final form around the 6th century AD. The Babylonian Talmud is more extensive and detailed than the Jerusalem Talmud, and it became the dominant version of the Talmud studied by Jews throughout the diaspora. The Babylonian Talmud is written in a combination of Hebrew and a more accessible form of Aramaic, and its discussions are often more elaborate and analytical.

The Talmud is structured as a series of commentaries and debates on the Mishnah, with the original text of the Mishnah at the center of the discussion. It also incorporates a wide range of other materials, including biblical interpretations (*midrash*), stories, ethical teachings, and legal precedents. The Talmudic discussions often explore complex legal and philosophical questions, reflecting the rabbis' deep engagement with the intricacies of Jewish law and tradition.

The study of the Talmud became the primary focus of Jewish education in the rabbinic academies, or *yeshivot*, that were established throughout the diaspora. Mastery of the Talmud was considered the highest achievement of a scholar, and its teachings influenced every aspect of Jewish life, from religious practice to civil law.

This important religious book also played a crucial role in unifying the diverse Jewish communities scattered across the Roman Empire and beyond. Despite the geographical distances and cultural differences that separated them, Jews throughout the diaspora could find common ground in the study and observance of the Talmudic law. The Talmud provided a shared framework for Jewish life, ensuring the continuity of Jewish tradition even in the face of dispersion and adversity.

One of the most significant centers was Babylonia, where a thriving Jewish community had existed since the Babylonian Exile. The Babylonian academies of Sura, Pumbedita, and Nehardea became the leading institutions of rabbinic scholarship, attracting students and scholars from across the Jewish world. In Babylonia, Jewish life was relatively stable and prosperous under the rule of the Sassanian Empire. The Jewish community enjoyed a degree of autonomy and was governed by the exilarch (*reish galuta*), a leader who represented the Jewish people to the Persian authorities. The exilarch, along with the heads of the Babylonian academies (the *geonim*), played a central role in the development and dissemination of Jewish law and tradition.

Meanwhile, in the western part of the Roman Empire, Jewish communities faced a more precarious existence. In places like Rome, Alexandria, and Carthage, Jews were often subject to discrimination, persecution, and forced conversions. Despite these challenges, Jewish communities continued to thrive, maintaining their religious practices and contributing to the broader cultural and intellectual life of the Roman world. The Jewish diaspora also extended beyond the boundaries of the Roman Empire. In Arabia, Yemen, Ethiopia, and the Caucasus, Jewish communities developed unique traditions and practices, often blending Jewish law with local customs. These far-flung communities were linked to the broader Jewish world through trade, pilgrimage, and the exchange of letters and texts.

One of the key contributions of the geonim was the development of *responsa* literature (*she'elot u-teshuvot*), a genre of Jewish legal writing in which the geonim responded to questions posed by Jewish communities across the diaspora. These *responsa* addressed a wide range of issues, from ritual observance and family law to commercial disputes and communal governance. The responsa literature played a vital role in maintaining the unity of Jewish law and practice, ensuring that Jews in different regions could adhere to a common legal framework. The geonim also oversaw the compilation of *siddurim* (prayer books), which standardized Jewish liturgy and made it more accessible to Jews who were no longer fluent in Hebrew. The *siddur* provided a structured format for daily prayers, Sabbath services, and festival observances, helping to preserve Jewish religious practice in the diaspora. The development of the siddur was particularly important in communities where the knowledge of Hebrew was declining, as it allowed Jews to maintain their connection to the traditional prayers and blessings.

One of the key areas of legal development during this period was the adaptation of Jewish law to the economic and social realities of diaspora life. For example, the prohibition against charging interest (*ribbit*) on loans, rooted in the Torah, posed a significant challenge for Jews engaged in trade and commerce in the Roman and later Islamic worlds. In response, the rabbis developed legal mechanisms such as the *heter iska*, a partnership agreement that allowed Jews to participate in commercial ventures while adhering to the prohibition against interest.

Another area of legal evolution was the adaptation of family law to the needs of diaspora communities. The Talmudic laws of marriage and divorce were often complicated by the geographical distances and differing legal systems of the host societies. The rabbis addressed these challenges by developing new procedures for issuing marriage contracts (*ketubot*) and for obtaining divorces (*gittin*) in accordance with Jewish law. These legal adaptations helped to maintain the integrity of Jewish family life and ensured that Jewish women and men could marry and divorce in a manner consistent with their religious traditions.

The rabbis of the diaspora also grappled with issues related to communal governance and authority. In the absence of a central Jewish authority, local Jewish communities developed their own systems of self-governance, often led by a rabbinical court (*bet din*) and a council of communal leaders. The rabbis provided legal and ethical guidance on issues such as communal taxation, charity, and the resolution of disputes, helping to maintain social cohesion and justice within the Jewish communities. The development of Jewish law during the early medieval period was also influenced by the interactions between Jewish and non-Jewish legal systems. In many regions, Jews lived under the authority of Islamic or Christian rulers, and they were often required to navigate between Jewish law and the legal codes of their host societies. The rabbis addressed these challenges by developing legal principles that allowed Jews to comply with the laws of the land (*dina de-malkhuta dina*) while remaining faithful to their religious obligations.

The study of the Talmud was not limited to the academies of Babylonia but spread to Jewish communities across the diaspora, particularly in Spain, North Africa, and southern France. The Talmudic scholars, or Talmudists, engaged in close textual analysis, debate, and commentary, seeking to uncover the deeper meanings and legal principles embedded in the Talmudic discussions. Their work led to the development of a vast body of Talmudic commentaries, which provided interpretations and explanations of the Talmudic text. One of the most significant contributions to Talmudic scholarship during this period was the work of Rabbi Shlomo Yitzhaki, known as Rashi (1040–1105 AD). Rashi's commentaries on the Talmud and the Hebrew Bible are considered foundational texts in Jewish scholarship. His clear and concise explanations made the Talmud more accessible to students and scholars, and his commentaries are still studied by Jewish students around the world today.

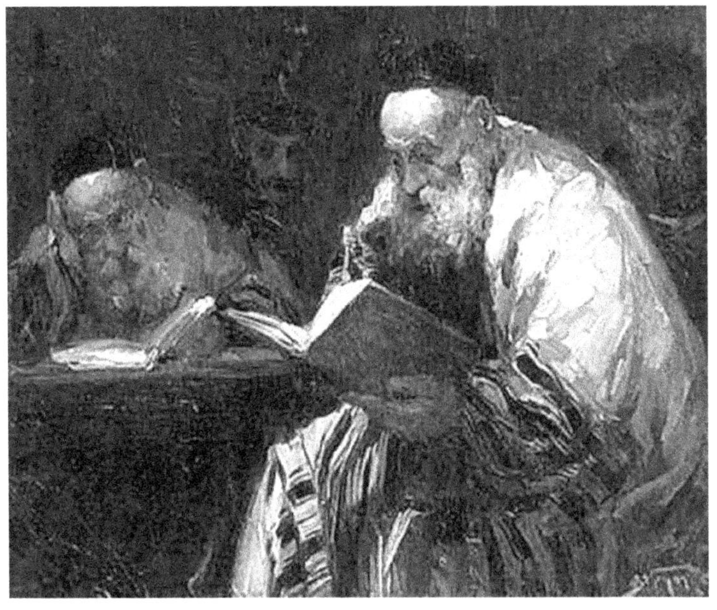

(Image: Adolf Behrman, Talmudysci, Public Domain)

In Spain, the Jewish community, known as the *Sephardim*, experienced a golden age of cultural and intellectual flourishing under Muslim rule. Jewish scholars in Spain made significant contributions to philosophy, science, medicine, and poetry, often engaging in dialogue with their Muslim and Christian counterparts. Figures such as Maimonides (*Rambam*) and Judah Halevi exemplify the intellectual achievements of the Sephardic Jewish community during this period.

In northern Europe, particularly in France and Germany, the Jewish communities, known as the *Ashkenazim*, developed their own distinct traditions of Talmudic study and religious practice. The Jewish academies of the Rhineland, in cities such as Mainz, Worms, and Speyer, became important centers of Jewish learning, producing scholars such as Rabbi Gershom ben Judah (960–1040 AD) and Rashi. The Ashkenazi tradition emphasized rigorous study of the Talmud and strict adherence to Jewish law, and it played a central role in the preservation of Jewish identity in Christian Europe.

As Jewish communities spread to new regions, they adapted to the local cultures and languages while maintaining their religious traditions and communal structures. The diversity of Jewish life in the diaspora enriched the Jewish tradition, leading to the development of distinct liturgical rites, customs, and legal interpretations. Despite these differences, Jews across the diaspora remained united by their shared commitment to the study of Torah and Talmud, their observance of Jewish law, and their enduring hope for the restoration of the Land of Israel.

Chapter 5
The Middle Ages

The medieval period was a time of significant transformation for Jewish communities as they navigated the complex and often challenging landscapes of Byzantine, Islamic, and Christian rule. The experiences of Jews during this era were marked by a mix of coexistence and conflict, intellectual and cultural achievements, and periods of prosperity followed by persecution and displacement. It is thus crucial to examine how Jewish communities adapted to and were influenced by the dominant cultures and religions of the regions in which they lived.

Jews in the Byzantine Era

The Byzantine Empire, with its capital in Constantinople, was a continuation of the Roman Empire in the East. Following the collapse of the Western Roman Empire in the 5th century AD, the Byzantine Empire became the dominant power in the eastern Mediterranean, exerting significant influence over the Jewish communities within its borders. Under Byzantine rule, Jews experienced a complex and often precarious existence. The empire, officially Christian, viewed Judaism as a rival and often heretical religion. This view was reflected in the legislation enacted by various Byzantine emperors, which frequently sought to restrict Jewish rights and limit their influence. For example, the Codex Theodosianus, a compilation of laws issued by Emperor Theodosius II in the early 5th century AD, included numerous provisions that discriminated against Jews. These laws prohibited Jews from holding public office, banned the construction of new synagogues, and restricted Jewish religious practices.

Despite these challenges, Jewish communities managed to survive and, in some cases, thrive under Byzantine rule. Jewish merchants played an essential role in the empire's economy, particularly in trade networks that connected the Mediterranean with the Near East. These merchants were often involved in the trade of spices, textiles, and other valuable commodities, and their economic activities helped sustain Jewish communities throughout the empire.

The intellectual life of Byzantine Jewry was also vibrant, particularly in cities such as Alexandria,

Antioch, and Constantinople. These cities were home to prominent Jewish scholars who contributed to the development of Jewish thought, particularly in the fields of Jewish law (*halakhah*), philosophy, and biblical exegesis. The influence of Hellenistic culture on Byzantine Jewry led to the integration of Greek philosophical concepts into Jewish thought, a process that would later have a profound impact on Jewish intellectual life in the Islamic world.

However, the relationship between the Byzantine state and its Jewish subjects was often strained. During periods of religious fervor or political instability, Jews were frequently scapegoated for the empire's troubles, leading to outbreaks of violence and persecution. One of the most significant episodes of anti-Jewish violence occurred during the reign of Emperor Heraclius in the early 7th century AD. Following a series of military defeats against the Persians, who had temporarily captured Jerusalem with the support of some Jewish factions, Heraclius ordered the forced conversion of Jews throughout the empire. This event marked one of the most severe persecutions of Jews in Byzantine history and left a lasting impact on the Jewish communities in the region.

The Byzantine Empire's approach to Jews was characterized by a combination of tolerance and repression, with periods of relative calm interspersed with episodes of harsh persecution. Despite these challenges, Jewish communities in the Byzantine Empire managed to maintain their religious and cultural identity, contributing to the broader Jewish diaspora's resilience.

During the earliest medieval period, there was one Judaic Kingdom that is often overlooked in historical literature. It was the **Kingdom of Himyar**, located in what is now modern-day Yemen, and it represents a unique chapter in the history of both the Arabian Peninsula and Judaism. It was one of the few pre-Islamic kingdoms in the region, thriving between the 4th and 6th centuries AD, and is notable for its rulers' conversion to Judaism. The kingdom's transformation into a Jewish state, its interactions with the Christian Byzantine Empire and the Christianized Kingdom of Aksum, and its eventual decline reflect a complex period of religious, political, and military upheaval.

The Kingdom of Himyar had its roots in southern Arabia, particularly in the southwestern part of the Arabian Peninsula, where the Himyarites established a strong state as early as the 2nd century BC. The Himyarites were part of a broader cultural and political landscape that included several other influential states, such as Saba' (Sheba), Ma'in, and Qataban, all of which were involved in controlling the lucrative incense trade routes that crossed the Arabian Peninsula. By the late 2nd century AD, the Himyarites had consolidated power in Yemen, establishing the Kingdom of Himyar, which expanded its influence over much of the region. Their economy was largely based on agriculture, and the kingdom benefited from the highly advanced irrigation systems that had been developed in the region, including the famous Marib Dam. Himyar also controlled key trade routes that connected the Arabian Peninsula with the Mediterranean, India, and East Africa, making it a wealthy and strategically important state. But the most significant and unique aspect of Himyar's history is the royal court's conversion to Judaism in the early 4th century AD. While the exact reasons for the conversion remain debated, several factors likely contributed to this development. The Jewish presence in southern Arabia was well-established by the 4th century, with Jewish communities living in various parts of the Arabian Peninsula, including Yemen. Jewish traders and missionaries likely played a role in spreading Jewish religious practices and beliefs throughout the region.

Moreover, the rise of Christianity in the Roman Empire, particularly after the conversion of Emperor Constantine in the early 4th century, placed the Himyarites in a religiously charged environment. Christianity had begun to spread in the region, particularly through the Kingdom of Aksum in neighboring Ethiopia. The conversion to Judaism may have been a political move by the Himyarite kings to assert their independence from the growing influence of Christian powers, particularly the Byzantine Empire and Aksum. By embracing Judaism, Himyar distanced itself from Christianization while fostering closer ties with Jewish communities across the region and beyond. One of the earliest kings associated with the conversion to Judaism was Tub'a Abu Karib As'ad, who ruled Himyar from around 390 to 420 AD. Although the exact details of his conversion remain unclear, Jewish sources and Arabian traditions both suggest that he played a key role in adopting Judaism as the state religion. According to Jewish tradition, Tub'a Abu Karib traveled to Yathrib (modern-day Medina) where he encountered Jewish scholars who impressed him with their monotheistic beliefs and scriptural knowledge. He is said to have embraced Judaism and brought Jewish religious practices back to his kingdom. Tub'a Abu Karib's reign is often seen as the starting point of Himyar's Jewish dynasty. Under his leadership, the kingdom expanded its influence over much of southern Arabia, and Judaism became an integral part of the state's identity. Himyar's Jewish kings, while maintaining traditional elements of Arabian kingship, patronized Jewish scholars, built synagogues, and promoted Jewish religious practices throughout the kingdom.

The adoption of Judaism in Himyar led to significant geopolitical tensions with neighboring Christian powers, particularly the Byzantine Empire and the Kingdom of Aksum. The Christianization of the Roman Empire, followed by the conversion to Christianity of the Aksumite kingdom under King Ezana in the early 4th century, created a religious divide between the Jewish Himyarites and their Christian neighbors. The Kingdom of Aksum, located across the Red Sea in modern-day Ethiopia, became a powerful adversary of Himyar. Aksum, which had strong ties with the Byzantine Empire, sought to spread Christianity throughout the region and frequently clashed with the Jewish Himyarite state. The religious tensions were exacerbated by economic and territorial disputes, particularly over control of the Red Sea trade routes.

A major turning point in the conflict between Himyar and Aksum came during the reign of the

Himyarite king Yusuf Dhu Nuwas, who ruled from around 517 to 525 AD. Dhu Nuwas, a fervent Jewish ruler, launched a series of campaigns against Christian communities in southern Arabia, including the massacre of Christians in the city of Najran in 523 AD. The massacre, in which many Christians were reportedly killed for refusing to renounce their faith, shocked the Christian world and provoked a strong response from the Byzantine Empire and Aksum.

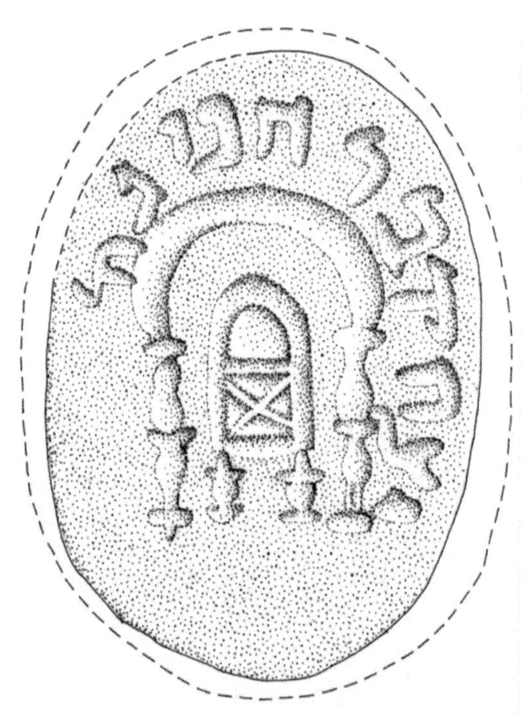

(Image: 04ring, Creative Commons Attribution 3.0)

The massacre at Najran triggered a series of events that led to the downfall of the Jewish Kingdom of Himyar. In response to the persecution of Christians, the Byzantine Emperor Justin I and the Christian King Kaleb of Aksum formed an alliance to overthrow Dhu Nuwas and end the Jewish rule in Himyar. Kaleb launched a military expedition across the Red Sea, supported by Byzantine ships and troops, to invade Himyar and restore Christian dominance in the region.

In 525 AD, Kaleb's forces successfully defeated Dhu Nuwas and his army, bringing an end to the Jewish Kingdom of Himyar. Dhu Nuwas is said to have died during the battle, either in combat or by committing suicide to avoid capture. Following his defeat, Kaleb installed a Christian vassal king, Sumyafa Ashwa, to rule over Himyar, and Christianity was re-established as the dominant religion in the region. Even though this kingdom was rather short-lived, it nevertheless marks an important part of the broader history of Judaism, the Jewish people, and Israel as a whole.

Jews within Islamic Nations

The rise of Islam in the 7th century AD brought about a dramatic shift in the political and religious landscape of the Middle East and North Africa. As the Islamic caliphates expanded, they incorporated vast territories that included significant Jewish populations, particularly in regions such as the Arabian Peninsula, Mesopotamia, Persia, Egypt, and later, Spain. Under Islamic rule, Jewish communities experienced a period of relative stability and flourishing, particularly during the early centuries of the Islamic Caliphates. The status of Jews under Islamic rule was defined by the concept of *dhimmi*, a legal status granted to non-Muslim "People of the Book," which included Jews and Christians. As dhimmis, Jews were allowed to practice their religion and maintain their communal institutions, but they were also subject to certain restrictions and obligations. These included the payment of a special tax known as the *jizya*, and they were required to adhere to various social and legal limitations, such as distinctive dress codes and restrictions on the construction of new synagogues.

Despite these restrictions, the early Islamic period was marked by significant advancements in Jewish religious and intellectual life. The Islamic Golden Age, which began in the 8th century, saw a flourishing of science, philosophy, medicine, and the arts, and Jewish scholars were active participants in this cultural and intellectual renaissance. The Jewish communities of Baghdad, Cairo, and Cordoba became major centers of Jewish learning, producing some of the most important Jewish scholars and thinkers of the medieval period. The relatively tolerant and intellectually vibrant atmosphere of the Islamic Caliphates allowed Jewish scholars to engage in fruitful exchanges with their Muslim and Christian counterparts, leading to significant developments in Jewish thought and practice.

One of the most important Jewish communities under Islamic rule was Babylonia (modern-day Iraq), which had already been a major center of Jewish scholarship during the Talmudic period. Under the Abbasid Caliphate (750–1258 AD), the Jewish academies of Sura and Pumbedita continued to be the leading centers of Jewish learning, and the geonim (heads of the academies) played a crucial role in the development and codification of Jewish law. The geonim's *responsa*, or legal rulings, were disseminated throughout the Jewish world, helping to unify Jewish practice across the diaspora.

In addition to Babylonia, Jewish communities in Spain, under Muslim rule, experienced a period of remarkable cultural and intellectual achievement. They produced some of the most renowned Jewish scholars of the medieval period, including Rabbi Moses ben Maimon (Maimonides), Rabbi Judah Halevi, and Rabbi Moses ben Ezra. These scholars made significant contributions to Jewish philosophy, poetry, and legal thought, and their works continue to be studied and revered by Jews today. The Jewish community in al-Andalus (Muslim Spain) was characterized by a high degree of integration into the broader society, with Jews playing prominent roles in the economic, political, and cultural life of the region. Jewish physicians, scientists, and administrators served in the courts of Muslim rulers, and Jewish merchants were active participants in the trade networks that connected the Islamic world with Europe, Africa, and Asia.

The relationship between Jews and Muslims in the Islamic world was generally marked by mutual respect and cooperation, although there were periods of tension and conflict. The relative tolerance of the early Islamic period contrasted sharply with the treatment of Jews in Christian Europe, where Jews were often subject to persecution and violence. However, the situation for Jews under Islamic rule was not always stable or secure. With rising anti-Semitism across Europe, the Jewish people were often targeted and falsely accused of various crimes. An infamous event that happened on December 30, 1066 was the Pogrom of Granada. At the time, Granada was one of the Muslim Taifa states that emerged following the collapse of the Caliphate of Córdoba in the early 11th century. These states were often culturally vibrant and relatively tolerant of religious minorities, including Jews and Christians, who were granted protection under Islamic law as dhimmis.

Despite their status as dhimmis, Jews held considerable influence in some of these kingdoms, with many serving as physicians, traders, and bureaucrats. Granada, in particular, had a significant Jewish community that had thrived under Muslim rule. The rise of the Zirid dynasty, which controlled Granada, saw the Jewish community enjoy unprecedented levels of prominence and power, largely due to the political and economic influence wielded by a single family: the Naghrela family. This family, originally from Córdoba, was headed by Samuel ibn Naghrela (993–1056), a polymath who rose to become the vizier, or chief advisor, to the Zirid ruler Habbus ibn Maksan. Samuel ibn Naghrela, also known as Shmuel HaNagid, was a highly educated scholar, poet, and military leader, in addition to being a devout Jew. He was widely respected for his wisdom and administrative skills, but his rise to such an influential position as a Jew in a Muslim court was highly unusual and stirred resentment among some of the local Muslim elite. Nevertheless, Samuel ibn Naghrillah served as vizier until his death in 1056, after which his son, Joseph ibn Naghrillah, succeeded him.

Joseph ibn Naghrillah (Yusuf ibn Naghrillah) inherited not only his father's position but also the resentment and hostility that had been building up against Jewish influence in Granada. While Joseph was an educated and capable leader, he lacked the diplomatic finesse of his father, and many in the Muslim aristocracy viewed him as a symbol of Jewish overreach. His leadership coincided with a period of political instability in Granada, and his growing influence was perceived as an abuse of power. Anti-Semitic rhetoric began to spread, fueled by both political rivals and religious leaders. These tensions reflected a broader wave of anti-Jewish sentiment that was emerging in various parts of the Islamic world at the time, often exacerbated by internal political struggles. Several factors contributed to this rising hostility:

1. **Economic Disparities:** While the Jewish community had prospered, many Muslims in Granada were struggling economically. This disparity fueled resentment, as Jews were often perceived as wealthy and privileged.

2. **Religious Tensions:** Islamic religious authorities were uncomfortable with the prominence of Jews in positions of power. Joseph ibn Naghrillah's role as vizier made him a target for clerics who believed that

non-Muslims should not hold such influence.

3. **Rumors and Slander:** False accusations began to spread that Joseph was plotting to betray the Muslim rulers of Granada and establish a **Jewish state**. While these accusations were baseless, they nonetheless inflamed tensions and justified the growing animosity toward the Jewish community.

4. **Power Struggles:** Internal rivalries within the Muslim court further stoked anti-Jewish sentiments. These rivalries came to a head in the months leading up to the massacre.

The violence erupted on December 30, 1066 (9 Tevet 4827 in the Jewish calendar) when a Muslim mob, incited by religious leaders and political figures, stormed the royal palace where Joseph ibn Naghrillah resided. They captured Joseph, dragged him out of the palace, crucified him, and mutilated his body. The mob then turned its wrath on the Jewish quarter of Granada and massacred as many as 4,000 Jews. The quarter was ransacked, with homes looted and synagogues destroyed. In the immediate aftermath of the pogrom, many surviving Jews fled Granada and sought refuge in other parts of Spain and North Africa. The Jewish community in Granada never fully recovered, and the events of 1066 cast a long shadow over Jewish-Muslim relations in the region.

The Pogrom of Granada served as a reminder of the precariousness of dhimmi status for Jews and Christians in Islamic lands. While they were allowed to live and practice their faiths, their position was always subordinate, and they were subject to the whims of the ruling class. The rise of figures such as Samuel and Joseph ibn Naghrillah, while exceptional, also illustrated the dangers of Jewish influence in a society where Muslims viewed non-Muslims as inferior. News of the pogrom spread to other Jewish communities across the Mediterranean, where it contributed to growing anxiety about the future of Jewish life in Islamic lands. The rise of more conservative Islamic movements, such as the Almohads in North Africa and Spain in the 12th century AD, led to increased pressure on Jewish communities to convert to Islam or face persecution, and many fled to more tolerant regions such as Egypt. As Christian forces began to reconquer territory from the Muslims during the Reconquista, Jews continued to face periods of persecution, culminating in their eventual expulsion from Spain in 1492.

Another key area where Jews lived in large numbers during the medieval period was the **Mamluk**

Sultanate (1250-1517 AD). The Mamluks, a military caste of Turkic and Circassian origin who ruled Egypt, Syria, and parts of the Arabian Peninsula, were Sunni Muslims who adhered to a relatively strict interpretation of Islamic law, particularly in terms of how they governed non-Muslims, including Jews and Christians. The legal framework was largely defined by the dhimmi system, under which Jews were granted a degree of religious autonomy but were subject to various restrictions intended to emphasize their subordinate status. These restrictions included the following:

- **Clothing Regulations:** Jews, along with Christians, were required to wear distinctive clothing or badges that marked their religious identity. This policy was rigorously enforced during different periods of Mamluk rule.

- **Synagogue Limitations:** While the Jews were allowed to maintain their places of worship, they were often restricted from building new synagogues or making repairs to existing ones without explicit permission. This regulation varied in enforcement based on the local authorities' disposition.

- **Occupational Restrictions:** Although many Jews served in various professional capacities in trade, medicine, and finance, some professions, particularly those involving the military or high administrative roles, were generally closed to non-Muslims.

Nevertheless, Jewish communities in major Mamluk cities such as Cairo, Damascus, and Aleppo played important roles in the region's economic and cultural life. Jewish merchants participated in local and international trade, connecting the Mamluk Sultanate to trade routes extending from Europe to India. Jewish moneylenders were also important, often facilitating credit for Muslim and non-Muslim clients alike, despite occasional resentment from the Muslim elite. The Jewish community also had skilled artisans, particularly in fields such as jewelry and textiles. In some periods, Jewish physicians enjoyed high status in the royal court and among the upper class. However, their economic role could be a double-edged sword, as wealth sometimes attracted accusations of exploiting the Muslim population, which occasionally led to increased taxation or outright persecution.

Despite their subordinate legal status, Jewish religious and intellectual life flourished in certain periods of the Mamluk Sultanate. Jewish communities maintained their religious schools (*yeshivot*) and cultural institutions, though they were careful not to attract undue attention from the authorities. The largest and most prominent Jewish community was in Cairo. Here there were various sects, such as Rabbanites and Karaites, the latter being a group that rejected the Talmudic traditions in favor of a strict adherence to the Hebrew Bible. Cairo was a major center of Jewish learning, and scholars such as the medieval philosopher and legal scholar Maimonides continued to influence Jewish thought during Mamluk times. A vast collection of documents, known as the Cairo Geniza, was found in a synagogue in Old Cairo (Fustat) and provided significant insight into the life of Jews under Mamluk rule.

Jews, like other non-Muslims, were often scapegoated for social or economic problems. One notable instance of persecution occurred in the late 14th century when Sultan Barquq (r. 1382–1399) issued decrees enforcing the wearing of distinctive clothing by Jews and limiting their economic and religious activities. Centuries later, the Jewish world was shocked by the infamous Damascus Blood

Libel of 1840, which had its roots in the tensions of the Mamluk era.

It is important to note that while Jews in the Mamluk Sultanate faced significant challenges, their treatment was generally better than that of Jews in Christian Europe at the same time, where violent expulsions, forced conversions, and massacres were more common. The Mamluk dhimmi system, although discriminatory, still allowed Jews to maintain their religious identity and community structures in relative peace for much of the period.

The end of Mamluk rule came in 1517 with the **Ottoman conquest** of Egypt and the Levant. Under Ottoman rule, the status of Jews improved in some ways, as the Ottomans adopted a more pragmatic approach to governing their diverse empire. The Ottoman sultans, recognizing the economic and administrative skills of their Jewish subjects, welcomed Jewish refugees from Spain and other parts of Europe, granting them protection and allowing them to establish new communities throughout the empire. Jewish merchants were active participants in the trade networks that connected the Mediterranean with the Middle East, Africa, and Europe, while Jewish artisans were renowned for their skills in textiles, metalwork, and other crafts.

In addition to their economic contributions, Jews in the Ottoman Empire made significant cultural and intellectual contributions. In Salonika (modern-day Thessaloniki), which became a major center for Sephardic Jews, Jewish scholarship flourished, particularly in the fields of *halakhah* (Jewish law) and *Kabbalah* (Jewish mysticism). Salonika's Jewish community was known for its vibrant religious life, with numerous synagogues, yeshivot, and religious schools that attracted students and scholars from across the Jewish world. Sephardic, Ashkenazic, and indigenous Jewish traditions blended to create a rich and diverse Jewish culture. Istanbul, too, thrived during the early centuries of Ottoman rule, benefiting from the empire's more lenient policies toward religious minorities.

Jewish Minorities in Christian Europe

The experience of Jews under Christian rule during the Middle Ages was markedly different from their experiences under Byzantine and Islamic rule. In Christian Europe, Jews were often viewed with suspicion and hostility, and their status was typically more precarious. Some Jewish communities were able to secure a degree of economic and social stability through their roles in commerce and finance. Jewish merchants played a crucial role in the trade networks that connected Europe with the

Middle East and Asia, while Jewish moneylenders provided essential financial services in a society where the Church prohibited Christians from charging interest on loans. However, Jews were often blamed for economic difficulties or accused of exploiting Christian society, and their roles made them vulnerable when rulers sought to cancel debts or confiscate Jewish wealth. The rise of Christianity as the dominant religion in Europe led to a theological and social environment that was often deeply antagonistic toward Jews, and this antagonism was reflected in the policies and actions of Christian rulers and the Church. The Church's teaching of Jews as "Christ-killers" further fueled anti-Jewish sentiment, leading to widespread discrimination, legal restrictions, and occasional outbreaks of violence.

One of the most significant turning points in the history of Jews in medieval Europe was the First Crusade (1096 to 1099 AD). As Crusader armies marched through Europe on their way to the Holy Land, they often attacked Jewish communities along the way, viewing them as enemies of Christianity. The massacres of Jews in cities such as Worms, Mainz, and Cologne were among the earliest and most brutal examples of anti-Jewish violence in medieval Europe. These events marked the beginning of a period of increasing persecution and marginalization for Jews in Christian Europe.

(Image: French Expulsion of Jews, 1182, Public Domain)

The medieval period also saw the emergence of various blood libels and accusations of ritual murder against Jews. These false accusations, which claimed that Jews used the blood of Christian children in religious rituals, were often used to justify violence against Jewish communities. The first recorded blood libel occurred in Norwich, England, in 1144 AD, and similar accusations spread throughout Europe in the following centuries, leading to numerous pogroms and expulsions. Despite these challenges, Jewish communities in Christian Europe also found ways to survive and even thrive in certain areas. Some Jewish communities, particularly in regions such as Provence, Northern Italy, and parts of Germany, became centers of Jewish learning and culture. Jewish scholars in these regions contributed significantly to the development of Jewish law, philosophy, and mysticism, often drawing on the intellectual currents of the broader Christian and Islamic worlds.

The 13th and 14th centuries were particularly difficult for Jewish communities in Christian Europe, marked by increasing persecution, expulsions, and forced conversions. One of the most significant expulsions occurred in 1290 AD when King Edward I of England issued the Edict of Expulsion, ordering all Jews to leave his kingdom. Similarly, in France, King Philip IV expelled the Jews in 1306 AD, although some were later allowed to return under specific conditions.

The Jews of Spain had one of the most diverse experiences of all the Jews in the diaspora. They had experienced a period of great flourishing during the tolerant Muslim rule of al-Andalus. This ushered in a "Golden Age" in Sepharad (the Hebrew-language name for the Iberian Peninsula), during which a distinct Sephardic identity emerged. However, by the late 14th and 15th centuries, growing religious intolerance and economic jealousy led to increasing pressure on Jewish communities. Under Christian rule, anti-Jewish sentiment was fueled by the preaching of figures such as Ferrand Martinez, a fanatical cleric who incited violence against Jews, leading to the pogroms of 1391, which devastated Jewish communities across Spain.

(Image: Grande Acedrex, Public Domain)

The culmination of this rising intolerance was the Alhambra Decree of 1492, issued by Ferdinand II of Aragon and Isabella I of Castile, which ordered the expulsion of all Jews from Spain. This decree marked the end of the once-flourishing Jewish community in Spain and forced tens of thousands of Jews into exile. Many sought refuge in the Ottoman Empire, while others fled to North Africa, Italy, and other parts of Europe. However, those who fled to neighboring Portugal faced further persecution when King Manuel I expelled Jews in 1496. Those who remained in Spain and converted to Christianity, known as *conversos* or *Marranos*, often continued to practice Judaism in secret, living in constant fear of persecution by the Inquisition.

The expulsion of Jews from Spain was a catastrophic event in Jewish history, but it also led to the dispersion of Sephardic Jews across the Mediterranean and beyond, where they established new communities and continued their cultural and intellectual traditions. The legacy of Sephardic Jewry, with its rich heritage of scholarship, poetry, and religious devotion, would continue to influence Jewish life for centuries to come.

The Jewish Pirates of the Caribbean

From these Jews in Spain and Portugal emerged a unique group, often completely overlooked in history. They are known as the Jewish Pirates of the Caribbean. Pirates have long been romanticized in popular culture, and tales of swashbuckling adventurers from the golden age of piracy abound, yet few are aware of these Jewish pirates who sailed the Caribbean during the age of exploration. These individuals played a remarkable role in the history of the region. Their story intertwines with the broader Jewish diaspora, European colonization, and the wars between imperial powers.

By the 16th century, many Sephardic Jews had fled to the New World, joining Spanish and Portuguese colonies in the Americas. Those who had converted to Christianity under duress and continued to practice their faith in secret became targets of the Spanish Inquisition, which operated in all Spanish colonies and territories. In this context, some Jews turned to piracy as a way to fight back against their persecutors and regain some of their wealth. It was a means of disrupting Spanish trade and weakening the empire responsible for their suffering and exile.

During the 16th and 17th centuries, the Caribbean became a hotbed of conflict between the Spanish, Portuguese, Dutch, French, and English powers.

As Spain and Portugal controlled much of the wealth flowing from the Americas, pirates and privateers – pirates licensed by governments to attack enemy ships – sought to plunder Spanish galleons laden with gold and silver. The Dutch and English, who were often at war with Spain, found Jewish pirates to be valuable allies in their struggles for dominance in the Caribbean.

With its many islands and remote coves, the Caribbean offered perfect locations for pirate bases. Jewish refugees from Europe found new homes in the region's burgeoning colonies. Islands such as Jamaica, Curacao, and Barbados became centers of Jewish life and pirate activity. Jamaica in particular stood out. When the English captured Jamaica from the Spanish in 1655, Jews from the Netherlands and elsewhere quickly moved to the island, seizing the opportunity to establish a community there. Jewish merchants became key players in Jamaica's economy, and some financed or even participated in piracy.

Several Jewish pirates rose to prominence during the golden age of piracy. While many of their names have been lost to history, a few stand out:

Moses Cohen Henriques:

Henriques worked alongside the notorious Dutch privateer Piet Hein. Together, they captured the Spanish treasure fleet in 1628, a massive blow to the Spanish Empire and one of the greatest hauls in pirate history. Henriques later established a pirate colony on the uninhabited island of Tortuga, off the coast of Haiti. Tortuga became a notorious base for pirate activity in the Caribbean, attracting buccaneers from across Europe. Henriques and his fellow Jewish pirates used the colony as a staging ground for attacks on Spanish shipping.

Samuel Pallache:

A Moroccan Jew and diplomat, Pallache worked as a privateer for the Dutch Republic, targeting Spanish ships. His career exemplified the fluid identities that many Jewish pirates held, combining their roles as merchants, diplomats, and privateers in an age of shifting alliances.

Ya'acob Curiel:

Curiel lived during the late 16th and early 17th centuries. Born in Portugal to a Jewish family that had converted to Christianity, Curiel eventually fled to the Dutch city of Amsterdam, which had become a center for Jewish refugees. He led a pirate fleet that targeted Spanish ships, and his family used their wealth and connections to help finance Dutch efforts against Spain.

David Abrabanel:

A descendent of the famous Abravanel family, David was a pirate who operated out of the Caribbean and the Mediterranean. He captured ships from various nations, focusing particularly on Spanish vessels. His family's prominence in Jewish history added to his legacy.

Jean Lafitte:

Though his Jewish heritage is debated, Lafitte himself stated that his parents were Sephardic Jews who fled and had to convert to Catholicism. Lafitte operated in the Gulf of Mexico in the early 19th century, and he played a crucial role in defending New Orleans against the British during the War of 1812.

Jewish piracy began to wane in the late 17th and early 18th centuries. Several factors contributed to this decline. The consolidation of European colonial powers in the Caribbean made piracy more difficult, as navies grew stronger and more organized. Additionally, many Jewish communities in the Caribbean became more established, with merchants and traders focusing on legitimate business opportunities rather than piracy. By the mid-18th century, the golden age of piracy had come to an end. However, the legacy of Jewish pirates lived on in the communities they helped build. In places like Jamaica, Curacao, and Barbados, Jewish families continued to thrive, contributing to the development of trade and culture in the Caribbean.

Other Jewish Minority Groups in Europe

Meanwhile, in Europe, other Jewish communities had also begun to establish themselves. Some significant communities emerged in Poland and Eastern Europe during the medieval period. The Jews of Poland, often referred to as the Litvaks or Galitzianers, benefited from the relatively tolerant policies of the Polish kings, who saw the economic and administrative benefits of encouraging Jewish settlement. Jewish communities in Poland and Eastern Europe developed their own distinct traditions, including a strong emphasis on communal autonomy and religious study.

In some regions, such as the Kingdom of Sicily, which came under Norman rule in the 11th century, Jews experienced a period of relative tolerance and prosperity. The Norman rulers, who were generally more pragmatic and less dogmatically Christian than their counterparts in northern Europe, recognized the economic and administrative value of their Jewish subjects. Jews in Sicily were involved in a wide range of economic activities, including trade, medicine, and finance, and they played a crucial role in the island's economic life.

Another important medieval Jewish community existed for centuries in Italy where they were known as *Italkim*. They represent one of the oldest Jewish communities in Europe, as Jewish settlement in Italy began in the 2nd century BC. Jewish communities flourished in cities such as Rome, Naples, and Venice during the Roman Empire. By the medieval period, these communities had established themselves as integral parts of Italian society, particularly in the urban centers of central and northern Italy. The Italkim had a unique position within the broader Jewish world, maintaining strong connections with Jewish communities across the Mediterranean while also developing distinct religious and cultural traditions. During the Middle Ages, the Byzantine Empire, Lombards, Normans, and various city-states and principalities all vied for control of different regions of Italy. This fragmented political environment meant that the experiences of Jewish communities depended on the local rulers and the prevailing social and religious attitudes.

(Image: Marco MARCUOLA, Un mariage juif, Creative Commons Attribution-Share Alike 4.0)

The Jews of Rome also occupied a unique position, given the city's status as the center of the Roman Catholic Church. Despite being under the direct jurisdiction of the papacy, the Jewish community in Rome was able to maintain its presence and traditions throughout the medieval period. This continuity was partly due to the historical significance of the Jewish community in Rome being one of the oldest in the world, and partly due to the Church's recognition of the Jews as a "protected" people, albeit in a subordinate and often marginalized role. Papal policies towards the Jews of Rome were inconsistent, varying from relatively benign tolerance to harsh restrictions, depending on the pope in power and the broader political and religious climate. Despite these fluctuations, the Jewish community in Rome managed to maintain its religious institutions, including synagogues and schools, and continued to engage in trade, banking, and other economic activities.

In northern Italy, cities such as Venice, Genoa, and Milan developed into powerful city-states with vibrant commercial economies. Jewish merchants were active in the trade networks that connected Italy with the rest of Europe and the Mediterranean, dealing in goods such as spices, textiles, and precious metals. The Republic of Venice, in particular, became a major center of Jewish life in the late medieval period. The Venetian government, while not entirely free from anti-Jewish sentiment, recognized the economic benefits of allowing Jews to reside and trade in the city and granted them certain privileges, including the right to practice their religion and manage their own affairs.

However, the medieval period saw the rise of anti-Jewish sentiment across Europe, often fueled by religious fervor and economic envy. This sentiment sometimes manifested in violence, such as the blood libels that occasionally erupted in Italian cities, where Jews were falsely accused of ritual murder. These accusations, which were rooted in deep-seated religious prejudices, often led to pogroms and the destruction of Jewish property. The Italkim were also subject to various legal restrictions that limited their rights and freedoms. These restrictions included sumptuary laws, which regulated what Jews could wear, and residency laws, which confined Jews to specific quarters of cities, known as ghettos. The most famous of these ghettos was the Venetian Ghetto, established in 1516, which became the model for similar Jewish quarters across Europe.

Despite these challenges, the Jews of Italy remained resilient, maintaining their religious and cultural identity while also contributing to the broader Italian society. Italy, with its well-established universities and intellectual culture, became a center of Jewish scholarship during the medieval period. Jewish scholars in Italy engaged in the study of Jewish texts, philosophy, and science, often in dialogue with the surrounding Christian and Muslim intellectual traditions. The Talmudic academies of Rome, Padua, and other Italian cities became important centers of learning, attracting students from across the Jewish world. Two notable scholars and rabbis of the period were Obadiah ben Abraham Bertinoro, a 15th-century rabbi who wrote a famous commentary on the Mishnah, and Leon of Modena, a 16th-century rabbi, writer, and musician who was active in Venice.

The Italkim were also involved in the broader cultural and intellectual movements of the Renaissance. Jewish scholars such as Elia del Medigo and Azariah dei Rossi translated and interpreted classical texts and engaged in debates with Christian scholars. The legacy of the Italkim is still evident today in the rich cultural and religious traditions they developed, which continue to influence Jewish life in Italy and beyond. Their contributions to Jewish scholarship, their engagement with broader intellectual movements, and their ability to maintain their identity in the face of adversity are a significant part of the broader story of the Jewish experience in medieval Europe.

The diverse experiences of Jews during the Middle Ages reflected the broader dynamics of the regions in which they lived, from the religious and political complexities of the Byzantine Empire to the cultural and intellectual vibrancy of the Islamic world, to the often-hostile environment of Christian Europe. It was a period marked by both flourishing and suffering. Despite the many challenges they faced, Jewish communities remained resilient, preserving their religious traditions, cultural identity, and intellectual heritage. The experiences of persecution, expulsion, and displacement that characterized much of Jewish life during this period left a lasting impact and shaped the collective memory and identity of the Jewish people as they entered the early modern era.

Chapter 6
The Jewish Enlightenment

The 18th and 19th centuries were marked by sweeping changes in politics, society, and culture. For Jewish communities across Europe, these centuries brought both unprecedented opportunities and profound dilemmas. On the one hand, the Enlightenment, with its emphasis on reason, individual rights, and secularism, challenged long-standing religious and social structures and norms. On the other hand, the push for civil rights and emancipation sought to integrate Jews into broader society as equal citizens. These developments gave rise to the *Haskalah*, or Jewish Enlightenment, a movement that sought to modernize Jewish life and thought and led to the emergence of new Jewish ideologies and movements that would have a lasting impact on Jewish history.

The Enlightenment itself was a complex and multifaceted intellectual movement that began in the late 17th century and reached its peak in the 18th century. Rooted in the scientific revolution and the writings of philosophers such as John Locke, Voltaire, and Immanuel Kant, the Enlightenment emphasized reason, skepticism of authority, and the pursuit of knowledge. Key thinkers of this movement questioned traditional religious doctrines and advocated the separation of church and state, the protection of individual rights, and the promotion of secular education.

The Haskalah began in Germany and Central Europe where Jews had long been marginalized and confined to specific occupations and neighborhoods. Leading figures of the Haskalah, known as Maskilim, sought to reform Jewish education, religious practice, and communal life to align with the ideals of the Enlightenment. They promoted the study of secular subjects, including science, literature, and philosophy, alongside traditional Jewish texts, and advocated for the use of vernacular languages in addition to Hebrew. One of the most influential figures of the Haskalah was Moses Mendelssohn (1729–1786), a German-Jewish philosopher who became a key proponent of integrating Jewish life with the broader intellectual and cultural currents of the Enlightenment. Mendelssohn argued that Jews could and should participate fully in European society without abandoning their religious and cultural identity. His writings, including his translation of the Hebrew Bible into German, were instrumental in encouraging Jews to engage with the wider world while also fostering a deeper understanding of their own religious heritage.

(Image: Moses Mendelson, Public Domain)

Mendelssohn's vision of Jewish integration and modernization was not without controversy. While many Jews embraced the ideals of the Haskalah, others viewed the movement with suspicion, fearing that it would lead to the erosion of traditional Jewish values and practices. This tension between tradition and modernity became a defining feature of Jewish life during the 18th and 19th centuries, as different communities and individuals grappled with the implications of the Enlightenment for their religious and cultural identity. His most famous work, *Jerusalem*, advocated for religious freedom and argued against the coercive power of religious institutions. He believed that Judaism, in its essence, was compatible with reason and that Jews could embrace Enlightenment values while maintaining their religious heritage. His philosophical contributions also extended beyond religion, as he engaged in debates with key thinkers of his time, such as Immanuel Kant and Gotthold Ephraim Lessing, the latter of whom depicted Mendelssohn in his play *Nathan the Wise*, a drama celebrating religious tolerance. Mendelssohn is often regarded as the father of modern Jewish philosophy and a pioneer in Jewish thought during this important period.

Jewish communities were also influenced by the French Revolution of 1789. Its rallying cry of "liberty, equality, fraternity" marked a turning point in the struggle for Jewish emancipation. In 1791, the National Assembly of France granted full citizenship to Jews, making France the first European country to do so. This landmark decision set a precedent that would inspire Jewish communities across Europe to demand similar rights and freedoms.

Prior to this decision, Jews in France, as in much of Europe, were subject to various restrictions and discrimination. They lived in semi-autonomous communities, often segregated from the rest of society, and faced limitations on their rights to own property, practice certain professions, or even move freely. This was especially true for Ashkenazi Jews in eastern France, such as in Alsace, who experienced a history of economic restrictions and social isolation. On the other hand, Sephardic Jews in southwestern France, particularly in cities such as Bordeaux, had enjoyed relatively more privileges, having settled in France after fleeing the Spanish and Portuguese Inquisitions. But as the revolutionaries now sought to establish a new French Republic based on the principles of equality and individual rights, the question of whether Jews, as a distinct religious and ethnic minority, could be integrated into the nation became part of broader discussions on civil liberties and human rights.

The topic of Jewish emancipation was hotly debated in the National Assembly. There were two primary opposing views. One side, led by figures such as the revolutionary priest Henri Grégoire and the Abbé Sieyès, argued that Jews should be granted full civil rights, just like other French citizens. They contended that equality before the law was a fundamental principle of the revolution and that Jews, if granted full citizenship, could be "regenerated" into useful and loyal members of society. On the other side, detractors expressed concerns about the perceived "separateness" of the Jewish community. Some argued that Jews could not be trusted to be loyal citizens because of their religious and economic ties and that their communal life was incompatible with the principles of the new republic. They feared that granting Jews citizenship would undermine French unity. However, the rising ideals of universal human rights, alongside practical considerations such as the Jewish population's involvement in trade and commerce, eventually swayed the decision in favor of emancipation. And so it was that on September 27, 1791, the National Assembly passed the decree that granted full citizenship to the Jews of France. The law read, *"The National Assembly, considering that the conditions necessary to be a citizen and to become a French citizen are to have attained the age of majority and to have taken the civic oath, decrees that all Jews who will take this oath shall enjoy the rights of French citizens."* This laid the foundation for the integration of Jews into French society and the broader acceptance of religious and ethnic minorities as equal participants in national life. It also signaled a broader European trend toward the modernization of state-minority relations and the application of Enlightenment principles of human rights.

The Path toward Emancipation

However, the path to full emancipation was far from straightforward. In many parts of Europe, Jews continued to face legal discrimination, social exclusion, and violent antisemitism. The responses to Jewish emancipation varied widely across the continent, reflecting the complex interplay of political, religious, and social forces in different regions. In Germany, for example, the process of emancipation was slow and uneven, with Jews gaining full civil rights only in 1871 with the unification of Germany under Otto von Bismarck. In the Austro-Hungarian Empire, Jews were granted equal rights in 1867 but continued to face significant social and economic barriers. The struggles for emancipation and integration led to the development of new Jewish ideologies and movements that sought to address the challenges of modernity while also preserving Jewish identity. One such movement was Reform Judaism, which emerged in early 19th-century Germany as a response to the pressures of assimilation. Reform Judaism sought to modernize Jewish religious practice by making it more compatible with contemporary values and lifestyles. This included changes such as the introduction of vernacular languages in synagogue services, the abandonment of certain traditional rituals, and a more flexible approach to religious law.

Reform Judaism quickly spread to other parts of Europe and to the United States, where it became a major force in the American Jewish community. However, the movement also sparked significant opposition from more traditionalist Jews, leading to the emergence of Orthodox Judaism as a distinct movement committed to preserving traditional Jewish law and practice. Orthodox Judaism emphasized the importance of religious practices such as the observance of the Sabbath, the dietary laws of *kashrut*, and the study of the Torah and Talmud. Orthodox Jews sought to maintain a distinct Jewish identity that was separate from the broader society, while also engaging with the challenges of modernity in a way that was consistent with traditional Jewish values.

The 19th century also saw the rise of new political ideologies that would have a profound impact on Jewish life. One of the most significant of these was Zionism, a movement founded by Theodor Herzl, that sought to establish a Jewish homeland in Palestine. Zionism emerged in the late 19th century as a response to the continued persecution and marginalization of Jews in Europe, particularly in Eastern Europe and Russia, where pogroms and antisemitic laws were widespread. The failure of the emancipation project to fully integrate Jews into European society led some Jews to conclude that the only solution was the establishment of a Jewish state where they could live in safety and dignity.

Zionism was not without its critics, both within and outside the Jewish community. Some Jews, particularly those who were more assimilated, viewed Zionism as a threat to their status as citizens of their respective countries. Others, particularly Orthodox Jews, opposed Zionism on religious grounds, arguing that the establishment of a Jewish state could only be achieved through divine intervention. Despite these debates, Zionism gained significant traction among Jews in Europe and the Middle East, laying the groundwork for the eventual establishment of the State of Israel in 1948.

The Quest for a New Homeland

As the 19th century progressed, the ideals of the Enlightenment and the push for emancipation continued to shape Jewish life across Europe. However, the situation was becoming increasingly complex, as new political, social, and economic forces began to challenge the status quo. The rise of nationalism, the spread of industrialization, and the emergence of modern antisemitism all had profound implications for Jewish communities, leading to new forms of Jewish identity and political organization. This second half of the chapter will explore these developments in greater detail, examining how Jewish communities responded to the changing world around them and how these responses laid the groundwork for the modern Jewish experience.

One of the most significant developments of the late 19th century was the rise of nationalism as a powerful force in European politics. Nationalism, with its emphasis on the idea of a shared national identity and the right of peoples to self-determination, had a profound impact on Jewish communities across Europe. For many Jews, particularly in Central and Eastern Europe, the rise of nationalism presented both opportunities and challenges. On the one hand, the idea of national self-determination resonated with Jews who were increasingly seeking to assert their own identity in the face of growing pressures to assimilate. On the other hand, nationalist movements often excluded or marginalized Jews, viewing them as outsiders who did not belong to the dominant national group.

In response to these challenges, Jewish thinkers and leaders began to explore new forms of Jewish nationalism that sought to reconcile the ideals of national self-determination with the realities of Jewish life in the diaspora. One of the most influential figures in this movement was Ahad Ha'am (1856–1927), a Jewish essayist and thinker who is often considered the founder of Cultural Zionism. Unlike Theodor Herzl's political Zionism, which sought to establish a Jewish state in Palestine, Ahad Ha'am's vision of Zionism was more focused on the cultural and spiritual renewal of the Jewish people. He argued that the establishment of a Jewish state should be seen not as an end in itself but as a means of revitalizing Jewish culture and identity in the face of the challenges posed by modernity. Ahad Ha'am's ideas had a significant influence on the development of Zionism, particularly among Jews in Eastern Europe, where the challenges of assimilation and antisemitism were particularly acute. However, the broader context of Jewish life in the late 19th century was shaped by a range of other factors, including the spread of industrialization and the associated social and economic changes. As Jews moved from rural areas to cities in search of new opportunities, they found themselves increasingly integrated into the fabric of modern European society. This process of urbanization and industrialization brought with it new opportunities for economic advancement, but it also exposed Jews to new forms of antisemitism and social exclusion.

(Image: Ahad Haam, Public Domain)

Another important development in this period was the rise of Socialism and other forms of political radicalism, which had a significant impact on Jewish life in Europe. The late 19th century was a time of great social and economic upheaval, as the spread of industrialization and urbanization led to the emergence of new social classes and the growth of political movements advocating for workers' rights and social justice. Many Jews, particularly in Eastern Europe, were drawn to these movements, seeing them as a way to address the economic and social inequalities that they faced.

The *Bund* (General Jewish Labour Bund in Lithuania, Poland, and Russia) was one of the most important Jewish socialist organizations of this period. Founded in 1897, the Bund sought to unite Jewish workers in the struggle for social and economic justice, while also advocating for the cultural and political rights of Jews as a distinct national minority. The Bund rejected both Zionism and assimilation, instead advocating for a form of Jewish autonomy within a socialist framework. The movement was particularly strong in the Pale of Settlement, the region of the Russian Empire where most of the empire's Jews were confined, and played a key role in the broader socialist movement in Russia and Eastern Europe.

The emergence of these new political and religious movements reflected the broader diversity of Jewish life in the late 19th century. While some Jews sought to integrate into broader society and embrace the opportunities of modernity, others sought to preserve their distinct identity and resist the pressures of assimilation. This diversity of responses was a testament to the resilience and adaptability of Jewish communities in the face of the profound changes that were sweeping across Europe. However, the late 19th century also saw the rise of a new and virulent form of antisemitism that posed a grave threat to Jewish communities across Europe. Unlike the religious antisemitism of the past, which was based on theological arguments about the supposed guilt of Jews for the death of Jesus, modern antisemitism was rooted in racist ideologies that portrayed Jews as an inherently inferior and dangerous race. This form of antisemitism was often linked to the broader nationalist and imperialist movements of the time, which sought to define national identity in terms of race and ethnicity.

The rise of modern antisemitism had a profound impact on Jewish life in Europe. In France, the Dreyfus Affair of the 1890s, in which a Jewish army officer was falsely accused of treason, exposed the deep-seated antisemitism that existed within

French society and led to widespread public debates about the role of Jews in the nation. In 1894, the French Army's counterintelligence unit discovered a letter, known as a bordereau, which indicated that secret military information had been passed to Germany, France's adversary at the time. Suspicion quickly fell on Captain Alfred Dreyfus, an artillery officer from Alsace, a region with a significant German-speaking population. Despite the flimsy evidence and the lack of clear motive, Dreyfus was convicted of espionage. At the time, France was experiencing a rise in nationalist and far-right sentiment, with growing resentment towards Jews, who were often scapegoated for the country's political and economic problems. Dreyfus became a target for those who believed that Jews could not be loyal to France. The far-right press, notably the newspaper *La Libre Parole*, led a campaign of hatred against Dreyfus, reinforcing stereotypes of Jews as traitorous and untrustworthy.

In 1896, evidence surfaced that cast doubt on Dreyfus's guilt. Major Georges Picquart, the head of French military intelligence, discovered that the real traitor was a French officer named Ferdinand Walsin Esterhazy. However, the army was reluctant to admit its mistake. When Picquart tried to bring the truth to light, he was silenced, demoted, and later imprisoned. Despite the efforts to suppress the evidence, a movement to exonerate Dreyfus began to take shape. Intellectuals, journalists, and politicians rallied to Dreyfus's cause, believing that his conviction was a miscarriage of justice. One of the most prominent supporters of Dreyfus was the novelist Émile Zola, who published an open letter titled "J'Accuse...!" in 1898. In this letter, Zola accused the French military and government of conspiracy and cover-up, sparking widespread public debate. In 1899, after intense public pressure, Dreyfus was brought back to France for a retrial. However, despite the mounting evidence in his favor, he was once again found guilty, though with "extenuating circumstances." This led to a public outcry, and in 1906, Dreyfus was finally exonerated by a civilian court and reinstated in the army. The affair, while legally resolved, left deep scars on French society. It highlighted the persistence of antisemitism and the challenges of maintaining democratic institutions in the face of populist and nationalist pressures.

In Germany, the rise of nationalist and antisemitic movements in the late 19th century laid the groundwork for the even more extreme forms of antisemitism that would emerge in the 20th century. In Eastern Europe, antisemitic violence, including pogroms in the Russian Empire, led to the mass emigration of Jews to the United States and other parts of the world. The hostility Jewish communities faced in Europe led to new forms of Jewish identity and political organization, including possibilities for Jewish self-determination.

Chapter 7
The Emergence of Zionism
and the Quest for Israel

Zionism represented a revolutionary idea: that the Jewish people, scattered across the globe, could once again establish a sovereign state in their ancient homeland of Palestine. At its core, Zionism was a response to centuries of Jewish marginalization and persecution in Europe, particularly in Eastern Europe, where the majority of the world's Jewish population lived at the time. In the Russian Empire, where millions of Jews lived in the Pale of Settlement, antisemitic violence and pogroms were frequent, leading to widespread fear and insecurity. The Pale of Settlement was a region in the western part of the Russian Empire where Jews were allowed to live. It was established in the late 18th century and existed until the early 20th century, as part of the empire's efforts to control and regulate the Jewish population. The area included parts of modern-day Poland, Lithuania, Ukraine, Belarus, and Moldova. It was created after the partitions of Poland (1772, 1793, 1795), when a large number of Jews came under Russian rule. Jews were generally prohibited from living outside the Pale without special permits, and their economic activities were often restricted. The Pale of Settlement subjected Jews to discrimination and poverty, as they were confined to economically underdeveloped regions and faced restrictions on property ownership, travel, and occupation. This led many Jews to seek emigration, particularly to the United States and Western Europe, during the late 19th and early 20th centuries.

In 1882, Tsar Alexander III introduced the infamous *May Laws*, which further exacerbated the situation. These laws, also known as the Temporary Rules, imposed severe restrictions on Jewish economic and social life, and many Jews began to question whether assimilation and integration were viable solutions to the "Jewish question." The laws were introduced in response to widespread anti-Jewish violence, specifically the pogroms that erupted after the assassination of Tsar Alexander II in 1881, which many people falsely blamed on Jewish radicals. There were three main provisions:

- Jews were prohibited from settling outside designated towns and villages within the Pale of Settlement, where Jews were already confined. This restriction essentially forced many Jews into overcrowded urban ghettos.

- Jews were barred from acquiring or renting land outside of these restricted areas. This prevented them from participating in agriculture or expanding their economic opportunities in rural areas.

- Jews were barred from various professions, and it became difficult for them to engage in trade or business outside Jewish communities, which contributed to their worsening poverty.

It was against this backdrop that the Zionist movement began to take shape. The term "Zionism" was coined by Nathan Birnbaum in 1890. It was derived from "Zion," a biblical term for Jerusalem and the Land of Israel. Zionism was not just a political movement; it was also a profound cultural and ideological shift that sought to redefine Jewish identity in modern terms. At its core, Zionism was based on the belief that Jews were not just a religious community but a nation with a right to self-determination and a homeland of their own.

One of the earliest and most influential proponents of Zionism was Theodor Herzl (1860–1904), an Austrian-Jewish journalist and playwright who is often regarded as the father of modern political Zionism. Herzl was deeply affected by the Dreyfus Affair in France, which exposed the deep-seated antisemitism that persisted in even the most liberal and enlightened societies of Europe. Herzl became convinced that the only solution was the establishment of a Jewish state that would ensure their security and survival. In 1896, he published "Der Judenstaat" (The Jewish State), a pamphlet in which he laid out his vision for the establishment of a Jewish homeland in Palestine. He believed that the establishment of such a state would not only provide a refuge for Jews fleeing persecution but also enable Jews to achieve national self-determination and take their place among the nations of the world.

Herzl's ideas resonated with many Jews who were disillusioned with the failed promises of emancipation and integration in Europe. In 1897, Herzl convened the First Zionist Congress in Basel, Switzerland, bringing together delegates from Jewish communities across Europe and beyond. The Congress marked the formal beginning of the Zionist movement and established the World Zionist Organization (WZO), which would serve as the central body coordinating Zionist activities and efforts to promote Jewish settlement in Palestine.

(Image: Herzl on a balcony, 1901, Public Domain)

At the Congress, Herzl famously declared, "In Basel, I founded the Jewish state. If I said this out loud today, I would be greeted by universal laughter. In five years, perhaps, and certainly in fifty years, everyone will recognize it." Herzl's vision of a Jewish state was met with both enthusiasm and skepticism within the Jewish community. While many embraced the idea, others, particularly within the more established Jewish communities of Western Europe, were wary of Zionism, fearing it would undermine their efforts to integrate into European society.

Despite these divisions, the Zionist movement continued to gain momentum, particularly among Jews in Eastern Europe, where the pressures of antisemitism and economic hardship were most acute. Zionism appealed to a wide range of Jews, from secular nationalists who sought to build a modern Jewish state, to religious Jews who saw the return to the Land of Israel as the fulfillment of biblical prophecy. The movement also attracted support from Jewish socialists and labor activists, who saw in Zionism an opportunity to build a just and egalitarian society.

The early Zionist movement was marked by a diversity of ideas and approaches. Herzl himself advocated for a diplomatic solution to the Jewish question, seeking the support of European powers for the establishment of a Jewish state in Palestine. He famously met with leaders such as Kaiser Wilhelm II of Germany and Sultan Abdul Hamid II of the Ottoman Empire in an effort to gain their backing for the Zionist cause. However, Herzl's efforts to secure international recognition for a Jewish state in Palestine were ultimately unsuccessful during his lifetime.

At the same time, other Zionist leaders emphasized the importance of practical efforts to settle Jews in Palestine and build the infrastructure of a future state. This approach, known as "practical Zionism," was championed by figures such as Menachem Ussishkin and Leo Motzkin, who believed that the establishment of a Jewish state would be achieved not through diplomacy, but through the gradual buildup of a Jewish presence in the Land of Israel. This included the purchase of land, the establishment of agricultural settlements, and the creation of Jewish institutions. The first significant wave of Jewish immigration to Palestine, known as the First Aliyah, took place between 1882 and 1903. During this period, approximately 25,000 to 30,000 Jews, mostly from Eastern Europe and Yemen, settled in Palestine. These early settlers faced numerous challenges, including harsh living conditions, disease, and hostility from the local

Arab population. Despite these difficulties, they succeeded in establishing several agricultural settlements, known as *moshavot*, which laid the foundation for future Jewish settlement in the region.

One of the most notable achievements of the First Aliyah was the establishment of the town of Petah Tikva in 1878, which became known as the "Mother of the Moshavot." The settlers of Petah Tikva, like those of other early Jewish settlements, sought to revive the ancient connection between the Jewish people and the land by working the soil and building a self-sustaining agricultural community. These early pioneers were driven by a deep sense of mission and a belief in the transformative power of labor and self-reliance.

The First Aliyah was followed by the Second Aliyah (1904–1914), which brought an additional 35,000 to 40,000 Jewish immigrants to Palestine, mostly from Eastern Europe. The Second Aliyah was characterized by a more ideological and socialist orientation, with many of the new immigrants influenced by the ideas of Labor Zionism. Labor Zionism, which became the dominant force within the Zionist movement, emphasized the importance of collective labor, social justice, and the creation of a Jewish working class as the basis for the future

Jewish state. One of the most influential figures of the Second Aliyah was David Ben-Gurion, who would later become the first Prime Minister of Israel. Ben-Gurion, like many of his contemporaries, believed that the Jewish state could only be built through the efforts of Jewish workers who would create a new, egalitarian society in the Land of Israel. The Second Aliyah saw the establishment of the first *kibbutzim*, or collective farms, which became a symbol of the pioneering spirit and socialist ideals of the early Zionist settlers.

As the Zionist movement gained momentum, it also began to attract the attention of the international community. The outbreak of World War I and the subsequent collapse of the Ottoman Empire, which had ruled Palestine for centuries, created a new geopolitical landscape in the Middle East. The British government, seeking to secure its interests in the region, issued the Balfour Declaration in 1917, which expressed support for *"the establishment in Palestine of a national home for the Jewish people."* The Balfour Declaration was a significant milestone in the history of Zionism, as it marked the first time that a major world power had officially endorsed the idea of a Jewish homeland in Palestine. It also included a clause emphasizing that *"nothing shall be done which may prejudice the civil and religious rights of existing non-Jewish communities in*

Palestine." Similarly, it mentioned that the rights and status of Jews in any other country should not be undermined by the creation of this homeland.

The Balfour Declaration was met with jubilation by many Jews, who saw it as a major step towards the realization of their national aspirations. However, it also raised serious concerns among the Arab population of Palestine, who feared that the establishment of a Jewish state would lead to their displacement and marginalization.

The early decades of the 20th century thus marked a critical period in the history of Zionism and the quest for a Jewish homeland. The movement, which had begun as a small and often marginalized initiative, had grown into a significant political force with international recognition and support. Nevertheless, the future of Israel and the Jewish people was heading into a new era. The period following World War I was filled with the complex dynamics between the Zionist movement, the British Mandate, the Arab population of Palestine, and the broader international community. These years were marked by intense political maneuvering, growing tensions between Jewish and Arab communities, and the tragic consequences of the Holocaust, which further intensified the urgency of establishing a Jewish state.

Following the issuance of the Balfour Declaration in 1917, Palestine came under British control as a mandate territory, formally recognized by the League of Nations in 1922. The British Mandate for Palestine was supposed to implement the provisions of the Balfour Declaration, which included the establishment of a "national home for the Jewish people" while ensuring that the civil and religious rights of the non-Jewish communities in Palestine were protected. However, the ambiguity of the Balfour Declaration and the conflicting promises made to both Jews and Arabs led to a situation of increasing tension and conflict.

The 1920s and 1930s were a period of significant Jewish immigration to Palestine, driven by rising antisemitism in Europe, particularly in Eastern Europe, and the opportunities presented by the Zionist movement. This wave of immigration, known as the Third Aliyah (1919–1923) and Fourth Aliyah (1924–1929), brought tens of thousands of Jews to Palestine. The new immigrants established new agricultural settlements, expanded urban centers, and contributed to the development of a modern economy. The *Histadrut* (General Federation of Labor) was established in 1920, representing workers and coordinating economic activities. It became a central institution in the *Yishuv* (the Jewish community in Palestine).

However, as Jewish immigration increased, so did the opposition from the Arab population, who viewed the influx of Jews and the expansion of Jewish settlements as a direct threat to their own national aspirations and economic interests. Tensions between Jews and Arabs erupted into violence on several occasions, most notably during the 1920 Nebi Musa riots and the 1921 Jaffa riots. These outbreaks of violence highlighted the deep-seated animosity between the two communities and foreshadowed the more intense conflicts that would arise in the coming years.

(Image: Resistance of Palestinian Men and Women, Public Domain)

In response to the growing unrest, the British government issued a series of White Papers which sought to limit Jewish immigration and land purchases in Palestine in an attempt to appease the Arab population. The most significant of these was the 1939 White Paper, which severely restricted Jewish immigration to 75,000 over the next five years and proposed the establishment of an independent Palestinian state within ten years, with Jews and Arabs sharing power. This policy was vehemently opposed by the Zionist movement, which saw it as a betrayal of the Balfour Declaration and a capitulation to Arab pressure.

The 1939 White Paper came at a time when European Jews were facing unprecedented persecution under Nazi rule. The rise of Adolf Hitler and the implementation of the Nuremberg Laws in Germany had already made life unbearable for Jews in many parts of Europe. The outbreak of World War II in 1939 and the subsequent conflicts led to another episode of great oppression and the decimating of the Jewish population of Europe. Many survivors were left traumatized and homeless.

The horrors of the Second World War had a profound impact on the Zionist movement and the broader international community. The sheer scale of the genocide underscored the urgent need for a safe haven for Jews, and Palestine, with its deep historical and religious significance, was now seen as the only viable option. However, the British restrictions on immigration made it nearly impossible for Jews to seek refuge in Palestine. This led to a wave of illegal immigration, known as *Aliyah Bet*, in which thousands of Jews attempted to enter Palestine despite the British blockade.

The post-war period saw a dramatic escalation in the struggle for Palestine. The Zionist movement, led by figures such as David Ben-Gurion, Chaim Weizmann, and Golda Meir, intensified its efforts to secure international support for the establishment of a Jewish state. The Jewish underground organizations in Palestine, including the Haganah (the main Jewish paramilitary organization), the Irgun, and the Lehi (Stern Gang), engaged in armed resistance against British rule, carrying out attacks on British military installations and infrastructure.

The most notorious of these actions was the King David Hotel bombing in 1946, carried out by the Irgun under the leadership of Menachem Begin. The bombing, which targeted the British administrative headquarters in Jerusalem, resulted in the deaths of 91 people, including British, Arab, and Jewish victims. The attack drew widespread condemnation but also highlighted the determination of the Jewish underground to force the British out of Palestine.

Amid growing international pressure and the escalating violence in Palestine, the British government announced its intention to withdraw from the mandate and referred the issue to the newly established United Nations. The UN formed a special committee, UNSCOP (United Nations Special Committee on Palestine), to investigate the situation and propose a solution. After extensive deliberations, UNSCOP recommended the partition of Palestine into two separate states – one Jewish and one Arab – with Jerusalem as an international city under UN administration.

The UN Partition Plan, formally known as UN General Assembly Resolution 181, was adopted on November 29, 1947, with 33 votes in favor, 13 against, and 10 abstentions. The plan allocated approximately 56% of the land to the Jewish state and 43% to the Arab state, with the remaining 1% comprising the international city of Jerusalem. The Jewish Agency, representing the Jewish community in Palestine, accepted the plan, despite its imperfections, as a basis for the establishment of a Jewish state. The Arab leadership, however, vehemently rejected the plan, viewing it as unjust and illegitimate, and vowed to resist its implementation by force.

The adoption of the UN Partition Plan set the stage for a violent and chaotic struggle for control of Palestine. As soon as the plan was announced, hostilities between Jews and Arabs intensified, with both sides preparing for the inevitable conflict that would follow the British withdrawal. The period between November 1947 and May 1948, known as the Civil War in Mandatory Palestine, was marked by fierce fighting, mass displacement of populations, and acts of terror committed by both Jewish and Arab forces.

The Haganah, the Irgun, and the Lehi launched a series of military operations aimed at securing Jewish control over the areas allocated to the Jewish state under the partition plan. One of the most significant of these operations was Operation Nachshon in April 1948, which aimed to break the Arab siege of Jerusalem and secure the road from Tel Aviv to the city. The operation was successful, allowing Jewish convoys to reach Jerusalem and supply the besieged Jewish population.

On the Arab side, the Arab Higher Committee, led by Haj Amin al-Husseini, called for a general strike and launched attacks on Jewish communities and convoys. The Arab Liberation Army, composed of volunteers from neighboring Arab countries, also joined the fight, seeking to prevent the establishment of a Jewish state. The conflict resulted in significant casualties on both sides, as well as the displacement of tens of thousands of Arabs and Jews from their homes. As the British prepared to withdraw from Palestine on May 15, 1948, the Jewish leadership in Palestine, led by David Ben-Gurion, moved forward with plans to declare the establishment of a Jewish state. On May 14, 1948, Ben-Gurion announced the creation of the State of Israel in a ceremony held at the Tel Aviv Museum. The Declaration of Independence, which Ben-Gurion read aloud, proclaimed the establishment of a Jewish state in the Land of Israel, to be known as the State of Israel. The declaration emphasized the historical and religious connection of the Jewish people to the land, as well as the right of the Jewish people to self-determination and sovereignty.

The declaration was met with jubilation among Jews in Palestine and around the world, but it also triggered an immediate and hostile response from the surrounding Arab states. On May 15, 1948, the day after the declaration, the armies of Egypt, Jordan, Syria, Lebanon, and Iraq invaded Israel, marking the beginning of the 1948 Arab-Israeli War (also known as the War of Independence). The war was a brutal and protracted conflict that would ultimately determine the fate of the nascent Jewish state.

Despite being outnumbered and outgunned, the newly formed Israel Defense Forces (IDF), composed of former Haganah fighters and other Jewish paramilitary groups, managed to repel the invading Arab armies and secure key territories. The Israeli forces were able to expand beyond the boundaries of the UN partition plan, capturing areas such as the Galilee, Negev, and parts of Jerusalem. The war also resulted in the displacement of a large number of Palestinian Arabs, an event that would become known as the *Nakba* (catastrophe) in Arab history.

The 1948 Arab-Israeli War ended with a series of armistice agreements signed in 1949 between Israel and its neighboring Arab states. These agreements established the Green Line, which would serve as the de facto borders of Israel until the Six-Day War in 1967. The war solidified the existence of the State of Israel, but it also left a legacy of unresolved conflict and hostility between Israel and the Arab world.

Ultimately, this period was marked by intense political and military struggles, profound human suffering, and the determination of the Jewish people to secure a homeland in the face of overwhelming odds. The creation of Israel in 1948 was a momentous event that fulfilled the aspirations of the Zionist movement, but it also set the stage for decades of conflict and tension in the region.

Chapter 8
Home at Last

The establishment of Israel brought with it a host of immediate challenges, both internal and external. Internally, the new state faced the daunting task of building a functioning government, economy, and society from scratch. Externally, Israel found itself in a region where its existence was vehemently opposed by its neighbors, leading to a state of constant tension and the ever-present threat of war.

One of the first and most pressing challenges for Israel was the absorption of a massive influx of immigrants. In the years following its founding, Israel saw the arrival of hundreds of thousands of Jews from Europe, the Middle East, and North Africa. Many of these immigrants were World War II survivors or refugees fleeing persecution in Arab countries. This wave of immigration, known as the Aliyah, was both a blessing and a burden for the young state. On one hand, it fulfilled the Zionist vision of gathering Jews from around the world to build a Jewish homeland. On the other hand, it placed enormous strain on Israel's limited resources, infrastructure, and economy.

The new immigrants arrived in a country that was still reeling from the effects of the 1948 war. Much of Israel's land was underdeveloped, and there was a severe shortage of housing, jobs, and basic services. The government, under the leadership of David Ben-Gurion, implemented a policy of austerity, known as the *tsena*, to manage the economic challenges. This period of rationing and economic hardship was marked by strict government control over the distribution of food, clothing, and other essential goods.

To address the housing crisis, the government embarked on a massive construction program, building new towns and cities across the country. These new settlements, often referred to as *ma'abarot* (transit camps), were initially temporary housing solutions for the waves of immigrants. Over time, many of these ma'abarot developed into permanent towns, contributing to the expansion of Israel's urban landscape.

The challenge of integrating such a diverse population into a cohesive society was another significant hurdle. Israel's population was a mosaic of different cultures, languages, and traditions, with Jews from Europe, known as Ashkenazim, and

Jews from the Middle East and North Africa, known as Mizrahim or Sephardim, forming the two largest groups. The Ashkenazi Jews, who were more established in the country and held most of the political and economic power, often looked down on the Mizrahi Jews, leading to social tensions and inequalities. This divide would persist for decades, shaping Israel's social fabric and domestic politics.

(Image: Declaration of the State of Israel, 1948, Public Domain)

The 1950s and 1960s were crucial decades for Israel as it sought to consolidate its statehood. During this period, Israel faced numerous external threats, most notably from its Arab neighbors, who continued to reject its existence and sought to undermine it through both military and diplomatic means. One of the most significant events was the Suez Crisis of 1956, also known as the Sinai Campaign. It began when Egypt, under the leadership of Gamal Abdel Nasser, nationalized the Suez Canal, a vital waterway for international trade. In response, Israel, along with Britain and France, launched a military campaign to seize control of the canal and the Sinai Peninsula. The operation was a military success for Israel, allowing it to capture the Sinai Peninsula and temporarily neutralize the threat posed by Egyptian forces. However, international pressure, particularly from the United States and the Soviet Union, forced Israel to withdraw from Sinai in exchange for guarantees of free passage through the Suez Canal and the deployment of a United Nations peacekeeping force in the region. The Suez Crisis highlighted Israel's military capabilities and its willingness to use force to defend its interests, but it also underscored the importance of international alliances and the need for Israel to deal diplomatically in Cold War politics, balancing its relations with the United States, the Soviet Union, and other global powers.

In the 1960s, Israel continued to grapple with the integration of its immigrant population and the development of its economy. The government pursued a policy of state-led economic development, investing heavily in infrastructure, industry, and agriculture. Key institutions such as the Histadrut (General Federation of Labor) and the Jewish Agency played central roles in the country's economic and social development. Israel's agricultural sector, in particular, became a symbol of national pride and a cornerstone of its economy. The development of modern agricultural techniques, including the pioneering of drip irrigation technology, transformed Israel's arid land into fertile fields, contributing to the country's self-sufficiency in food production and its emergence as a leader in agricultural innovation.

A Generation of War

Internationally, Israel continued to face hostility from its Arab neighbors, culminating in the Six-Day War of 1967. In the months leading up to the war, Egypt, under Nasser's leadership, had mobilized its military forces in the Sinai Peninsula, expelled the UN peacekeeping forces, and blockaded the Straits of Tiran, cutting off Israel's access to the Red Sea. These actions, combined with aggressive rhetoric from Arab leaders calling for Israel's destruction, created a sense of imminent threat in Israel.

In response to these provocations, Israel launched a preemptive strike on June 5, 1967, targeting the air forces of Egypt, Syria, and Jordan. The operation was a resounding success, with Israel's air force achieving near-total air superiority within the first few hours of the conflict. Over the next six days, Israeli forces advanced rapidly on multiple fronts, capturing the Sinai Peninsula and the Gaza Strip from Egypt, the West Bank (including East Jerusalem) from Jordan, and the Golan Heights from Syria. The outcome of the Six-Day War was a decisive victory for Israel, dramatically altering the balance of power in the Middle East. Israel's territorial gains more than tripled the size of the country, giving it control over strategically important areas and significantly enhancing its security. The capture of East Jerusalem, in particular, had profound symbolic and religious significance, as it brought the Old City and the Western Wall, one of Judaism's holiest sites, under Israeli control. However, the war also set the stage for ongoing conflict. The occupation of the West Bank, Gaza Strip, and Golan Heights brought millions of Palestinians under Israeli military control, creating a complex and contentious situation that continues to this day. The war also intensified the Arab-Israeli conflict, leading to increased militancy among Palestinian groups and the rise of the Palestine Liberation Organization (PLO) under the leadership of Yasser Arafat.

The international community, including the United Nations, responded to the war with calls for Israel to withdraw from the territories it had occupied. UN Security Council Resolution 242, passed in November 1967, called for the "*withdrawal of Israeli armed forces from territories occupied in the recent conflict*" and the recognition of the right of every state in the region to live in peace within secure and recognized borders. The resolution laid the groundwork for future peace negotiations, but its ambiguous language and differing interpretations by Israel and the Arab states have led to ongoing disputes over its implementation.

The Six-Day War marked a turning point in Israel's history, transforming it into a regional military power and solidifying its position as a key player in the Middle East. The war also had a profound impact on Israeli society, boosting national morale and fostering a sense of unity and pride. However, it also sowed the seeds of future conflicts, as the occupation of the Palestinian territories became a central issue in the Israeli-Palestinian conflict and a source of international controversy.

The years following the Six-Day War were marked by increasing tensions and intermittent conflicts between Israel and its Arab neighbors. These culminated in the Yom Kippur War of 1973, another pivotal moment in Israel's history. On October 6, 1973, during Yom Kippur – the holiest day in Judaism – Egypt and Syria launched a coordinated surprise attack on Israel. Egyptian forces crossed the Suez Canal into the Sinai Peninsula, while Syrian troops advanced into the Golan Heights. The initial phase of the war saw significant Arab gains, as Israel was caught off guard and struggled to mobilize its reserves. The situation was dire, with Israeli forces facing the possibility of a catastrophic defeat. However, Israel's military quickly regrouped and mounted a counteroffensive. In the Sinai, Israeli forces, under the command of General Ariel Sharon, executed a bold maneuver by crossing the Suez Canal, encircling the Egyptian Third Army, and threatening Cairo. In the north, Israeli troops pushed Syrian forces back from the Golan Heights and advanced toward Damascus. By the time a ceasefire was brokered by the United States and the Soviet Union on October 25, Israel had regained much of the territory lost in the early days of the war and was in a strong position militarily.

(Image: 143th Division during Yom Kippur War, IDF Spokesperson's Unit, Creative Commons Attribution-Share Alike 3.0)

The Yom Kippur War strained Israel's relationship with the United States, as Washington pressured Israel to accept a ceasefire and engage in peace negotiations. This led to the Camp David Accords in 1978, where Israel, under Prime Minister Menachem Begin, and Egypt, led by President Anwar Sadat, negotiated a peace treaty. In exchange for peace, Israel agreed to return the Sinai Peninsula to Egypt. This was the first time an Arab state officially recognized Israel's right to exist. While the Camp David Accords were a significant diplomatic achievement, the peace treaty with Egypt isolated Israel from much of the Arab world and was met with skepticism and opposition within Israel itself, where many saw the relinquishment of the Sinai as a dangerous concession. Moreover, the war and its aftermath deepened the divide within Israeli society, particularly regarding the occupation of the Palestinian territories and the future of the West Bank and Gaza Strip.

The 1980s and 1990s saw Israel grappling with the ongoing challenges of maintaining security while seeking a lasting peace with its neighbors. The situation in the occupied territories became increasingly volatile, with the rise of the Palestinian Intifada in 1987, a widespread uprising against Israeli rule in the West Bank and Gaza Strip. The Intifada, marked by protests, strikes, and violent clashes between Palestinian youths and Israeli soldiers, brought the Palestinian issue to the forefront of international attention and put pressure on Israel to seek a resolution. In response, the Israeli government began to explore the possibility of negotiations with the Palestinians. These efforts culminated in the Oslo Accords of 1993, a landmark agreement between Israel and the Palestine Liberation Organization (PLO), led by Yasser Arafat. The Oslo Accords, brokered by Norway and signed on the White House lawn, represented the first direct, face-to-face agreement between the two parties. Under the terms of the

Oslo Accords, Israel and the PLO recognized each other's right to exist and agreed to a framework for future negotiations aimed at achieving a two-state solution. The accords called for the establishment of a Palestinian Authority with limited self-rule in parts of the West Bank and Gaza, while final-status issues, including the borders of a future Palestinian state, the status of Jerusalem, and the right of return for Palestinian refugees, were to be negotiated in subsequent talks.

The Oslo Accords were hailed by many as a breakthrough in the Israeli-Palestinian conflict and a significant step toward peace. However, the agreement was also highly controversial and deeply divisive, both in Israel and among the Palestinians. In Israel, the accords were met with fierce opposition from right-wing and religious groups, who saw the concessions made to the Palestinians as a threat to Israel's security and territorial integrity. The assassination of Prime Minister Yitzhak Rabin in 1995 by a Jewish extremist underscored the deep divisions within Israeli society over the peace process. On the Palestinian side, the Oslo Accords were seen by many as a betrayal of the Palestinian cause, particularly because they did not immediately address the key issues of statehood, refugees, and Jerusalem. The continued expansion of Israeli settlements in the West Bank and the perceived failure of the peace process to deliver tangible improvements in the lives of ordinary Palestinians fueled resentment and disillusionment, leading to the outbreak of the Second Intifada in 2000.

The Second Intifada, which lasted until 2005, was characterized by suicide bombings, military operations, and a dramatic increase in violence between Israelis and Palestinians. The conflict had a devastating impact on both sides, leading to thousands of deaths and deepening the mistrust and animosity that had long plagued the region. In response, Israel implemented a series of security measures, including the construction of a controversial security barrier along the West Bank, which Israel argued was necessary to prevent terrorist attacks. While the barrier significantly reduced the number of suicide bombings, it also further complicated the situation on the ground, as it often cut through Palestinian communities, leading to widespread criticism from the international community and accusations that it was an attempt to unilaterally define Israel's borders.

During this period, Israel also faced challenges on its northern border with Lebanon, where the militant group Hezbollah launched attacks against Israeli targets. The situation culminated in the 2006 Lebanon War, a month-long conflict between Israel and Hezbollah that resulted in significant destruction in both Lebanon and northern Israel. While Israel achieved some of its military objectives, the war exposed the limitations of its military power and led to a reevaluation of its strategy in dealing with non-state actors such as Hezbollah.

Despite these challenges, Israel continued to pursue peace initiatives, most notably the 2005 Gaza Disengagement, in which Israel unilaterally withdrew its settlers and military forces from the Gaza Strip. This was intended to reduce friction between Israelis and Palestinians and create conditions for renewed peace talks. However, the subsequent takeover of Gaza by the militant group Hamas and the continued firing of rockets into Israel from Gaza led to further conflicts, including the Gaza War of 2008-2009 and subsequent military operations. The ongoing conflict with the Palestinians and the broader regional instability have posed significant challenges to Israel's security and diplomatic efforts. Nevertheless, Israel has sought to maintain its strategic alliances, particularly with the United States, while also exploring new partnerships in the region. In recent years, Israel has achieved a series of diplomatic breakthroughs, including the Abraham Accords of 2020, which normalized relations with several Arab countries, including the United Arab Emirates, Bahrain, Sudan, and Morocco. These agreements, brokered by the United States, represent a significant shift in the Middle East's geopolitical landscape and offer the potential for a new era of cooperation between Israel and its Arab neighbors.

While Israel's history has been marked by conflict and challenges, the country has also achieved remarkable success in various fields. From its early days, Israel placed a strong emphasis on education, research, and innovation, which have become key drivers of its economic growth and global influence. Israel's high-tech sector has earned the country the nickname "Startup Nation," reflecting its status as a global leader in technology. Israeli companies have made significant contributions to fields such as cybersecurity, medical technology, and agriculture, with many startups achieving international success. The government's support for research and development, combined with a highly educated and entrepreneurial population, has helped Israel become one of the world's most technologically advanced economies. Israel has also made significant strides in the creative arts. Israeli literature, film, and music have gained international recognition, reflecting the country's vibrant and diverse culture. The Hebrew language, which was revived and modernized in the 19th and 20th centuries, serves as a unifying force for Israel's Jewish population and plays a central role in the country's cultural identity.

Economically, Israel has transformed from a struggling, agrarian society into a modern, industrialized nation with a high standard of living. The country's economy has diversified over the decades, with significant growth in sectors such as technology, finance, and tourism. Despite periods of inflation and recession, Israel has managed to maintain steady economic growth, attracting foreign investment and establishing itself as a key player in the global economy.

Israel's relationships with other countries are shaped by its history, security concerns, and its ongoing conflict with the Palestinians. While Israel has faced diplomatic challenges, particularly regarding its policies in the occupied territories, it has also forged strong alliances and partnerships with countries around the world. The relationship between Israel and the United States remains a cornerstone of Israel's foreign policy. The United States provides significant military and economic aid to Israel and has been a key supporter of Israel in international forums. The two countries share a deep bond based on shared democratic values, strategic interests, and a commitment to Israel's security. In recent years, Israel has sought to expand its diplomatic and economic ties with other regions, including Asia, Africa, and Latin America. Israel's expertise in technology and innovation has opened new avenues for cooperation, particularly in areas such as agriculture, water management, and renewable energy.

However, Israel continues to grapple with the challenges of achieving peace and security in a volatile region. The ongoing conflict with the Palestinians remains a central issue, with no easy solutions in sight. The conflict with Palestine that erupted in late 2023 is one of the most complex disputes in modern history. Of course, the conflict is centered on the territorial, political, and national claims over the land that both the Palestinians and the Israelis consider their own. In particular, the Israeli settlements in East Jerusalem and on the West Bank are a key source of tension. The Palestinians see this as illegal encroachments on land that was intended for a future Palestinian state, while the Israelis assert historical and security-related claims over these areas.

The clash takes place on multiple levels, including military confrontations, political stalemates, and major social upheaval. Gaza, which has been under the control of the Islamist group Hamas since 2007, has instigated repeated violence. Hamas does not recognize Israel's right to exist, and the latter has engaged in several armed confrontations with them. These conflicts usually result in significant casualties, with Israel conducting airstrikes in response to rocket attacks from Gaza. The humanitarian situation in Gaza is dire, made worse by blockades imposed by Israel and Egypt, both of which restrict the movement of goods and people, creating shortages of essential supplies. Jerusalem is also a focal point of the conflict, where tensions are high and conflicts often erupt in the area of the Al-Aqsa Mosque, known to Jews as the Temple Mount. Both Israel and Palestine claim Jerusalem as their capital city, even though Israel controls it entirely following the 1967 war.

International efforts to broker peace in this conflict have yielded mixed results so far. The United States plays a leading role in the mediation, supporting Israel but promoting peace talks. However, peace plans have consistently faltered due to disagreements over key issues such as borders, the right of return for Palestinian refugees, and the status of Jerusalem. Meanwhile, regional players such as Egypt, Jordan, and more recently the Gulf States, have engaged in diplomatic efforts, with varying degrees of success. For now, the conflict is ongoing, and the entire world hopes for peace and an acceptable solution to this long-lasting feud.

Chapter 9
Preserving Culture through the Hardships

When talking about the history of a nation and its people, one needs to look past the wars and the conflicts, past the exiles and pogroms, and beyond the politics and economy. What lies beyond is a nation's culture, its artistic development, and its contributions to those more beautiful aspects of our history. From ancient times to the modern era, Jewish cultural and artistic expression has reflected a deep connection to faith, history, and the changing circumstances of the Jewish people across different regions and time periods.

The origins of Jewish culture and art can be traced back to the biblical period (around 1200 BC to 500 BC) when the foundations of Judaism were laid. During this time, cultural expression was deeply intertwined with religion, and much of what is known comes from the Torah (the first five books of the Hebrew Bible), which served not only as a religious text but also as a cultural and ethical guide.

The most significant artistic and architectural undertaking of this period was the construction of the First Temple in Jerusalem under King Solomon around the 10th century BC. This temple became the spiritual and cultural center of the Jewish people. It housed the Ark of the Covenant and was decorated with intricate carvings, golden artifacts, and finely crafted utensils used in religious rituals. These religious objects, such as the menorah (a seven-branched candelabrum), are essential symbols of Jewish artistic heritage.

Jewish culture from its earliest days was primarily focused on the written word. The Hebrew Bible, composed over several centuries, is a monumental piece of literature that includes a variety of genres — law, history, poetry, prophecy, and wisdom literature. The Psalms, for instance, are profound examples of religious poetry, while the Song of Songs reflects the artistic use of metaphor and allegory in biblical poetry.

(Image: Song of Songs Rothschild Mahzor, Public Domain)

In 586 BC, the Babylonians destroyed the First Temple and the Jewish people were exiled to Babylon. After their return, they rebuilt the Temple (known as the Second Temple), and Jerusalem once again became the religious and cultural hub. During this period, synagogues emerged as places of communal worship and study. These buildings did not feature works of art in deference to the Jewish prohibition of idolatry, but they were often adorned with mosaics and architectural flourishes in the Hellenistic or Roman style. After the conquests of Alexander the Great in the 4th century BC, Jewish communities had more exposure to Greek culture. This period produced works such as the Book of Ecclesiastes and The Wisdom of Solomon, which are strongly influenced by Hellenistic philosophy. Jewish artists, while adhering to monotheistic principles, began to incorporate Greco-Roman artistic techniques, particularly in architecture and coinage.

After the destruction of the Second Temple by the Romans in 70 AD, the Jewish people were dispersed across the Roman Empire, marking the beginning of the Jewish diaspora. As Jewish communities settled in different regions, their cultural and artistic expressions diversified. Jewish art during the Middle Ages was influenced by the surrounding cultures in Europe, North Africa, and the Middle East. For instance, in Islamic lands, Jews produced illuminated manuscripts of religious texts such as the Haggadah (which narrates the story of Passover). These manuscripts featured intricate decorations, often borrowing stylistic elements from Islamic art, such as geometric patterns and floral motifs. In Christian Europe, Jews faced restrictions on their participation in the broader cultural sphere, but they nonetheless contributed to the production of illuminated Hebrew Bibles. One famous example is the Sarajevo Haggadah, created in Spain in the 14th century, which features beautiful illustrations of biblical scenes.

Jewish music in the medieval period continued to develop through the chanting of psalms and prayers in synagogues. The cantillation marks (notations for chanting the Torah and other scriptural readings) became a central aspect of Jewish liturgical practice. Jewish communities across different regions developed unique musical traditions, influenced by the cultures they lived in; Sephardic Jews in Spain and North Africa, for example, blended traditional Hebrew songs with Arabic and Moorish melodies. The medieval period was also a golden age for Jewish philosophy and poetry. Maimonides (1135–1204) blended Jewish thought with Aristotelian philosophy, producing works such as *The Guide for the Perplexed*, which remains one of the most important philosophical texts in Jewish history. Jewish poets such as Judah Halevi and Solomon Ibn Gabirol produced deeply spiritual and philosophical poetry, often expressing themes of exile, longing for Zion, and devotion to God.

As European Jews faced increasing persecution during the late medieval period, particularly in Spain with the expulsion of Jews in 1492, many Jewish communities moved eastward to places such as the Ottoman Empire, Poland, and Lithuania. During the early modern period, Jewish art was largely centered around religious items – Torah scrolls, marriage contracts (*ketubot*), and ritual objects such as *mezuzot* (parchments for doorposts) and Hanukkah lamps. Jewish craftsmen often combined elements of local artistic styles with Jewish symbolism. The Renaissance also saw the growth of Jewish mysticism, particularly through the Kabbalah, which had a profound influence on Jewish artistic and spiritual life. Kabbalistic teachings inspired new forms of artistic expression, including mystical interpretations of the Hebrew alphabet and sacred geometry.

In the 18th century, the rise of Hasidism in Eastern Europe fostered a new approach to Jewish culture, one that emphasized joyous worship and personal connection to the divine. Hasidic music and dance became central aspects of Jewish life, with *niggunim* (wordless melodies) expressing spiritual longing and ecstasy.

The Haskalah (Jewish Enlightenment) movement of the 18th and 19th centuries encouraged a blending of Jewish and European intellectual life. Figures such as Moses Mendelssohn promoted the study of secular subjects alongside traditional Jewish texts, leading to a flourishing of Jewish literature, science, and philosophy. This period also saw the emergence of new Jewish art forms, for example, the painting of Jewish life in Eastern Europe by artists such as Maurycy Gottlieb and Isidor Kaufmann.

In the late 19th and early 20th centuries, many Jewish artists contributed to modern art movements in Europe and America. Marc Chagall, one of the most famous Jewish artists of the 20th century, blended elements of Jewish folklore, Russian village life, and avant-garde art in his vibrant, dreamlike paintings. Jewish artists also played key roles in the Bauhaus and Abstract Expressionist movements.

Another aspect of Jewish cultural life was the rise of Yiddish theater in Eastern Europe and later in New York City. Playwrights such as Sholem Aleichem and actors such as Molly Picon brought

Jewish stories to the stage, blending humor, tragedy, and social commentary. Jewish filmmakers, particularly in Hollywood, have had a profound impact on global cinema, with figures such as Steven Spielberg becoming icons of the film industry.

In the 20th century, Jewish literature flourished in multiple languages – Hebrew, Yiddish, German, Russian, and English. Famous writers include Isaac Bashevis Singer, Sholem Aleichem, and Saul Bellow, who explored themes of exile, identity, faith, and modernity, often drawing on their Jewish heritage.

However, the establishment of the State of Israel in 1948 marked a significant turning point in Jewish cultural history. Modern Israeli art and culture have been shaped by the experiences of immigration, the Holocaust, and the creation of a new Jewish state. Israeli artists, musicians, writers, and filmmakers have produced a vibrant body of work that reflects the complexities of Israeli society. Israeli music blends influences from Middle Eastern, European, and American traditions. Similarly, modern Hebrew literature has flourished, and well-known authors include Amos Oz, David Grossman, and Agnon (the first Israeli to win the Nobel Prize for Literature). Israeli cinema, too, has gained international acclaim for its exploration of both political and personal themes.

Jewish art and culture have played a vital role in preserving the identity, history, and traditions of the Jewish people throughout centuries of dispersion and challenges. From ancient religious texts to contemporary artistic expression, these cultural elements express resilience, continuity, and connection to their roots. They not only reflect Jewish spirituality and heritage but also serve as a source of strength and unity, ensuring that Jewish values remain an enduring legacy.

Conclusion

The history of Israel is a narrative of survival, perseverance, and adaptation. Throughout its ancient history, Israel was shaped by the geopolitics of the Near East. Situated at the crossroads of Africa, Asia, and Europe, the land of Israel was subject to the influence of great civilizations – Egypt, Assyria, Babylon, Persia, Greece, and Rome. Each empire left its mark, but the people of Israel, beginning with the early Israelites of the Iron Age, developed a distinct identity and consolidated their kingdom. The religious and ethical contributions of Israel's early prophets, lawgivers, and kings laid the foundation of a belief system that has had an indelible impact on world history.

The destruction of the First Temple and the Babylonian exile in 586 BC was a pivotal moment in Jewish history, signaling the transition from a land-based kingdom to a people bound by shared faith, culture, and covenant. The return from exile and the construction of the Second Temple allowed for the re-establishment of religious and political autonomy under Persian rule, though this autonomy was often fragile. The Hellenistic period, followed by Roman domination, tested Israel's identity, culminating in the revolts that led to the destruction of the Second Temple in 70 AD and the dispersal of the Jewish people. These events transformed Judaism from a temple-based religion into a diasporic faith centered on study, prayer, and community.

The Jewish diaspora, stretching across the Roman and Byzantine Empires, North Africa, and beyond, became a defining feature of Jewish life for nearly two millennia. During this time, Jewish communities adapted to the diverse environments in which they lived, from the Mediterranean to the Middle East to Europe. They sometimes enjoyed periods of relative peace and stability, as seen during the Golden Age of Jewish culture in Muslim Spain, and at other times faced severe persecution, as during the Crusades and the Inquisition. Throughout the Middle Ages, Jews in Christian Europe and under Islamic rule were both insiders and outsiders, at once vital to the economic and cultural life of their host countries but also frequently marginalized or scapegoated. The resilience of Jewish communities in maintaining their religious traditions, intellectual pursuits, and communal structures ensured the survival of Judaism through centuries of adversity. The

Talmudic academies of Babylon, the rise of Kabbalistic thought in medieval Spain, and the proliferation of yeshivot (Jewish schools) across Europe underscored the vibrancy of Jewish intellectual and spiritual life even in exile.

By the modern era, the forces of nationalism, secularism, and the Enlightenment began to reshape Jewish life, as they did much of the world. Jewish thinkers and leaders grappled with questions of identity, modernity, and the possibilities of integration into European society. However, the rise of antisemitism, culminating in the horrors of the Holocaust, reinforced the vulnerability of Jewish existence without a state of their own. The events of the 20th century would make the question of Zionism – the movement for the re-establishment of a Jewish homeland – an existential one. The establishment of the State of Israel in 1948 marked the culmination of a centuries-long yearning for a return to their ancestral land. However, it also initiated a new chapter of conflict, as it exacerbated tensions with the Arab populations already residing in the region. Historical grievances, political ambitions, and religious convictions have led to recurring wars and intermittent violence, making security and survival the cornerstones of Israel's national policy.

Despite these challenges, Israel has evolved into a vibrant, dynamic democracy with a thriving economy, cutting-edge technological industries, and a rich cultural life. The modern state is a global center for Jewish religious and cultural renewal, while also being a multi-ethnic society that includes not only Jews from across the world but also Arab citizens, Druze, and other minority groups. This diversity has enriched Israeli culture but has also posed significant challenges in terms of social cohesion, equality, and the integration of different communities.

The ongoing Israeli-Palestinian conflict remains one of the most intractable issues of modern times. Solutions to establishing peace, security, and justice continue to elude both sides, despite numerous efforts at resolution. The question of how to balance Israel's identity as a Jewish state with the democratic values it espouses remains a central issue in its domestic politics. These unresolved tensions reflect the broader challenges of nationhood in a region fraught with religious, ethnic, and political divisions.

As Israel moves further into the 21st century, it faces several complex challenges. Demographic changes, both within Israel and in the broader Jewish diaspora, pose questions about the future direction of Jewish identity. The rise of global antisemitism in recent years has once again highlighted the precariousness of Jewish life outside of Israel. Meanwhile, the role of religion in Israeli society – whether in politics, education, or public life – continues to spark intense debate. But despite these uncertainties, Israel's story is one of remarkable achievement. In a relatively short time, it has developed into a modern nation that continues to play an outsized role on the world stage. Its contributions to science, technology, culture, and international diplomacy have made Israel an indispensable part of the global community.

Israel is a civilization that has profoundly shaped the religious, moral, and cultural fabric of the world. From the monotheistic revolution of the ancient Israelites to the modern State of Israel's innovations in technology and diplomacy, the influence of Israel extends far beyond its geographical borders. Israel remains a symbol of resilience and renewal, constantly navigating the tensions between tradition and modernity, between survival and flourishing.

It carries with it the weight of its extraordinary legacy – one of hope, survival, and a relentless pursuit of peace in a world that remains as complex and challenging as ever.

References

Books:

- Avi-Yonah, M. (2001). *A history of Israel and the Holy Land.* A&C Black.

- Behrman, Adolf. *Talmudysci.* Retrieved from Wikimedia Commons, Public Domain. Available at: https://upload.wikimedia.org/wikipedia/commons/5/55/Adolf_Behrman_-_Talmudysci.jpg.

- Benbassa, E. (2000). *Sephardi Jewry: A History of the Judeo-Spanish Community, 14th-20th Centuries.* University of California Press.

- Blatner, D. and Falcon, T. (2011). *Judaism For Dummies.* John Wiley & Sons.

- Bright, J. (1981). *A history of Israel.* SCM Press.

- Efron, J. (2016). *The Jews: A History.* Taylor & Francis.

- Goldberg, H. E. (1996). *Sephardi and Middle Eastern Jewries: History and Culture in the Modern Era.* Indiana University Press.

- Golden, J. M. (2009). *Ancient Canaan and Israel: An Introduction*. Oxford University Press, USA.
- Isserlin, B. S. J. (1998). *The Israelites*. Thames & Hudson.
- Kamm, A. (1999). *The Israelites: An Introduction*. Psychology Press.
- Kritzler, E. (2009). *Jewish Pirates of the Caribbean: How a Generation of Swashbuckling Jews Carved Out an Empire in the New World in Their Quest for Treasure, Religious Freedom –- and Revenge*. Knopf Doubleday Publishing Group.
- Liverani, M. (2014). *Israel's history and the history of Israel*. Routledge.
- McNutt, P. (1999). *Reconstructing the Society of Ancient Israel*. Westminster John Knox Press.
- Reich, B. (2008). *A brief history of Israel*. Infobase Publishing.
- Rosenberg, A. (2003). *The Yom Kippur War*. The Rosen Publishing Group, Inc.
- Satlow, M. L. (2006). *Creating Judaism: History, Tradition, Practice*. Columbia University Press.
- Shindler, C. (2013). *A History of Modern Israel*. Cambridge University Press.

- Smith, M. S. (2002). *The Early History of God: Yahweh and Other Deities of Ancient Israel*. Wm. B. Eerdmans Publishing.
- Stein, L. (2013). *The Making of Modern Israel: 1948-1967*. Polity Press.

Images and Media:

- 143th Division during Yom Kippur War. IDF Spokesperson's Unit. Licensed under Creative Commons Attribution-Share Alike 3.0 Unported. Retrieved from Wikimedia Commons. Available at: https://upload.wikimedia.org/wikipedia/commons/c/ca/143th_Division_during_Yom_Kippur_War._I.jpg. License available at: https://creativecommons.org/licenses/by-sa/3.0/
- Ahad Haam. Retrieved from Wikimedia Commons, Public Domain. Available at: https://upload.wikimedia.org/wikipedia/commons/a/a5/Ahad_Haam.jpg.
- Behrman, Adolf. *Talmudysci*. Retrieved from Wikimedia Commons, Public Domain. Available at: https://upload.wikimedia.org/wikipedia/commons/5/55/Adolf_Behrman_-_Talmudysci.jpg.

- Carl Schleicher. *Jüdische Szene 1*. Retrieved from Wikimedia Commons, Public Domain. Available at: https://upload.wikimedia.org/wikipedia/commons/b/b9/Carl_Schleicher_J%C3%BCdische_Szene_1.jpg.
- Declaration of the State of Israel, 1948. Retrieved from Wikimedia Commons, Public Domain. Available at: https://upload.wikimedia.org/wikipedia/commons/3/36/Declaration_of_State_of_Israel_1948.jpg.
- French Expulsion of Jews, 1182. Retrieved from Wikimedia Commons, Public Domain. Available at: https://upload.wikimedia.org/wikipedia/commons/9/99/1182_french_expulsion_of_jews.jpg.
- Grande Acedrex. Retrieved from Wikimedia Commons, Public Domain. Available at: https://upload.wikimedia.org/wikipedia/commons/5/5e/Grande-acedrex.jpg.
- Herzl on a Balcony, 1901. Retrieved from Wikimedia Commons, Public Domain. Available at: https://upload.wikimedia.org/wikipedia/co

mmons/c/c4/Herzl_on_a_balcony_1901.j
pg.
- Israel-2013-Aerial View of Masada. Andrew Shiva. Retrieved from Wikimedia Commons. Available at: https://upload.wikimedia.org/wikipedia/co mmons/1/14/Israel-2013-Aerial_21-Masada.jpg.
- KAnana.gif. Released into the public domain by the copyright holder. Retrieved from Wikimedia Commons. Available at: https://upload.wikimedia.org/wikipedia/co mmons/d/d4/KAnana.gif.
- Kebara 2 skeleton replica. Dedicated to the public domain under the Creative Commons CC0 1.0 Universal Public Domain Dedication. Retrieved from Wikimedia Commons. Available at: https://upload.wikimedia.org/wikipedia/co mmons/f/fb/Kebara_2_skeleton_replica.jp g.
- Marco MARCUOLA. *Un mariage juif (titre attribué), Venise, vers 1780.* Licensed under Creative Commons Attribution-Share Alike 4.0 International. Retrieved from Wikimedia Commons. Available at: https://upload.wikimedia.org/wikipedia/co mmons/f/f0/Marco_MARCUOLA%2C

<u>Un mariage juif %28titre attribu%C3%A 9%29 Venise%2C vers 1780.jpg</u>. License available at: <u>https://creativecommons.org/licenses/by-sa/4.0/</u>

- Marble Head of Alexander the Great, Beth Shean. 2nd-1st Century BC. Retrieved from Wikimedia Commons, Public Domain. Available at: <u>https://upload.wikimedia.org/wikipedia/commons/thumb/a/a0/Marble_Head_of_Al exander_the_Great%2C_Beth_Shean%2C_2nd-1st_Century_BC_%2828348265957%29.jpg/1365px-Marble_Head_of_Alexander_the_Great%2 C_Beth_Shean%2C_2nd-1st_Century_BC_%2828348265957%29.jpg</u>.

- Moses Mendelson. Retrieved from Wikimedia Commons, Public Domain. Available at: <u>https://upload.wikimedia.org/wikipedia/commons/1/1c/Moses_Mendelson_P716007 3.JPG</u>.

- Pompey the Great, Museo Archeologico Nazionale. Retrieved from Wikimedia Commons, Public Domain. Available at:

https://upload.wikimedia.org/wikipedia/co
mmons/a/a4/%28Venice%29_Pompey_th
e_Great%2C_Museo_Archeologico_Nazio
nale.jpg.

- Resistance of Palestinian Men and Women.
  Retrieved from Wikimedia Commons,
  Public Domain. Available at:
  https://upload.wikimedia.org/wikipedia/co
  mmons/b/b5/Resistance_of_Palestinian_
  men_and_women.png.

- Schnorr von Carolsfeld, Julius. *Bibel in
  Bildern*. 1860. Retrieved from Wikimedia
  Commons, Public Domain. Available at:
  https://upload.wikimedia.org/wikipedia/co
  mmons/e/e8/Schnorr_von_Carolsfeld_Bi
  bel_in_Bildern_1860_029.png.

- Song of Songs Rothschild Mahzor.
  Retrieved from Wikimedia Commons,
  Public Domain. Available at:
  https://upload.wikimedia.org/wikipedia/co
  mmons/1/12/Song_of_songs_Rothschild_
  mahzor.jpg.

- The Talmud Students. Retrieved from
  Wikimedia Commons, Public Domain.
  Available at:
  https://upload.wikimedia.org/wikipedia/co
  mmons/5/5b/The_Talmud_students.jpg.

- Weller, Edward. *The Kingdoms of Judah and Israel.* Retrieved from Wikimedia Commons, Public Domain. Available at: https://commons.wikimedia.org/wiki/File: Edward Weller, The Kingdoms of Judah and Israel

FREE BONUS FROM HBA: EBOOK BUNDLE

Greetings!

First, thank you for reading our books.

Now, we invite you to join our VIP list. As a welcome gift we offer the History & Mythology eBook Bundle below for free. Plus, you can be the first to receive new books and exclusives! Remember it's 100% free to join.

Simply click the link below to join.

https://www.subscribepage.com/hba
Keep up to date with us on:
YouTube: History Brought Alive
Facebook: History Brought Alive
www.historybroughtalive.com

www.ingramcontent.com/pod-product-compliance
Lightning Source LLC
Chambersburg PA
CBHW051825150726
47998CB00001B/297